AMERICAN ARTISTS INCORPORATED

WWW.AMERICANARTISTSINCORPORATED.COM

ALL RIGHTS RESERVED. NO PART OF THIS BOOK MAY BE REPRODUCED OR TRANSMITTED IN ANY FORM OR BY ANY ELECTRONIC OR MECHANICAL MEANS, INCLUDING PHOTOCOPYING, RECORDING OR BY ANY INFORMATION STORAGE AND RETRIEVAL SYSTEM, WITHOUT WRITTEN PERMISSION FROM THE PUBLISHER.

THE ENCLOSED MATERIAL IS INTELLIGENT PROPERTY OF AMERICAN ARTISTS INCORPORATED. ANY REPRODUCTION OF THIS BOOK IN ANY FORM IS PROHIBITED BY COPYWRITE LAWS.

EDITED BY KATHY HAMMOND GESKE

PRINTED OCTOBER 2020

REPRINTED DECEMBER 2020

BUSINESS NAME

PROFIT AND LOSS STATEMENT – DATE:		TO	
REVENUES			
	$		$
	$		$
	$		$
	$		$
	$		$
TOTAL REVENUES	$		
COST OF GOODS SOLD	$		
GROSS PROFIT	$		
OPERATING EXPENSES			
ADVERTISING	$		
AMORTIZATION	$		
AUTOMOBILE EXPENSES	$		
CHARITABLE CONTRIBUTIONS	$		
DEPRECIATION	$		
EQUIPMENT RENTAL	$		
INSURANCE	$		
INTEREST EXPENSE	$		
LICENSES	$		
OFFICE SUPPLIES	$		
OFFICER COMPENSATION	$		
PAYROLL EXPENSES	$		
RENT	$		
TELEPHONE	$		
TRAVEL & ENTERTAINMENT	$		
UTILITIES	$		
WASTE DISPOSAL	$		
TOTAL OPERATING EXPENSE	$		
NET ORDINARY INCOME	$		
OTHER INCOME	$		
OTHER EXPENSES	$		
NET INCOME	$		

BUSINESS NAME

PROFIT AND LOSS STATEMENT – DATE: TO		
REVENUES		
	$	$
	$	$
	$	$
	$	$
	$	$
TOTAL REVENUES	$	
COST OF GOODS SOLD	$	
GROSS PROFIT	$	
OPERATING EXPENSES		
ADVERTISING	$	
AMORTIZATION	$	
AUTOMOBILE EXPENSES	$	
CHARITABLE CONTRIBUTIONS	$	
DEPRECIATION	$	
EQUIPMENT RENTAL	$	
INSURANCE	$	
INTEREST EXPENSE	$	
LICENSES	$	
OFFICE SUPPLIES	$	
OFFICER COMPENSATION	$	
PAYROLL EXPENSES	$	
RENT	$	
TELEPHONE	$	
TRAVEL & ENTERTAINMENT	$	
UTILITIES	$	
WASTE DISPOSAL	$	
TOTAL OPERATING EXPENSE	$	
NET ORDINARY INCOME	$	
OTHER INCOME	$	
OTHER EXPENSES	$	
NET INCOME	$	

BUSINESS NAME

PROFIT AND LOSS STATEMENT – DATE: TO			
REVENUES			
	$		$
	$		$
	$		$
	$		$
	$		$
TOTAL REVENUES	$		
COST OF GOODS SOLD	$		
GROSS PROFIT	$		
OPERATING EXPENSES			
ADVERTISING	$		
AMORTIZATION	$		
AUTOMOBILE EXPENSES	$		
CHARITABLE CONTRIBUTIONS	$		
DEPRECIATION	$		
EQUIPMENT RENTAL	$		
INSURANCE	$		
INTEREST EXPENSE	$		
LICENSES	$		
OFFICE SUPPLIES	$		
OFFICER COMPENSATION	$		
PAYROLL EXPENSES	$		
RENT	$		
TELEPHONE	$		
TRAVEL & ENTERTAINMENT	$		
UTILITIES	$		
WASTE DISPOSAL	$		
TOTAL OPERATING EXPENSE	$		
NET ORDINARY INCOME	$		
OTHER INCOME	$		
OTHER EXPENSES	$		
NET INCOME	$		

BUSINESS NAME

PROFIT AND LOSS STATEMENT – DATE:		TO	
REVENUES			
	$		$
	$		$
	$		$
	$		$
	$		$
TOTAL REVENUES	$		
COST OF GOODS SOLD	$		
GROSS PROFIT	$		
OPERATING EXPENSES			
ADVERTISING	$		
AMORTIZATION	$		
AUTOMOBILE EXPENSES	$		
CHARITABLE CONTRIBUTIONS	$		
DEPRECIATION	$		
EQUIPMENT RENTAL	$		
INSURANCE	$		
INTEREST EXPENSE	$		
LICENSES	$		
OFFICE SUPPLIES	$		
OFFICER COMPENSATION	$		
PAYROLL EXPENSES	$		
RENT	$		
TELEPHONE	$		
TRAVEL & ENTERTAINMENT	$		
UTILITIES	$		
WASTE DISPOSAL	$		
TOTAL OPERATING EXPENSE	$		
NET ORDINARY INCOME	$		
OTHER INCOME	$		
OTHER EXPENSES	$		
NET INCOME	$		

BUSINESS NAME

PROFIT AND LOSS STATEMENT - DATE:			TO
REVENUES			
	$		$
	$		$
	$		$
	$		$
	$		$
TOTAL REVENUES	$		
COST OF GOODS SOLD	$		
GROSS PROFIT	$		
OPERATING EXPENSES			
ADVERTISING	$		
AMORTIZATION	$		
AUTOMOBILE EXPENSES	$		
CHARITABLE CONTRIBUTIONS	$		
DEPRECIATION	$		
EQUIPMENT RENTAL	$		
INSURANCE	$		
INTEREST EXPENSE	$		
LICENSES	$		
OFFICE SUPPLIES	$		
OFFICER COMPENSATION	$		
PAYROLL EXPENSES	$		
RENT	$		
TELEPHONE	$		
TRAVEL & ENTERTAINMENT	$		
UTILITIES	$		
WASTE DISPOSAL	$		
TOTAL OPERATING EXPENSE	$		
NET ORDINARY INCOME	$		
OTHER INCOME	$		
OTHER EXPENSES	$		
NET INCOME	$		

BUSINESS NAME

PROFIT AND LOSS STATEMENT – DATE: TO				
REVENUES				
	$			$
	$			$
	$			$
	$			$
	$			$
TOTAL REVENUES		$		
COST OF GOODS SOLD		$		
GROSS PROFIT		$		
OPERATING EXPENSES				
ADVERTISING		$		
AMORTIZATION		$		
AUTOMOBILE EXPENSES		$		
CHARITABLE CONTRIBUTIONS		$		
DEPRECIATION		$		
EQUIPMENT RENTAL		$		
INSURANCE		$		
INTEREST EXPENSE		$		
LICENSES		$		
OFFICE SUPPLIES		$		
OFFICER COMPENSATION		$		
PAYROLL EXPENSES		$		
RENT		$		
TELEPHONE		$		
TRAVEL & ENTERTAINMENT		$		
UTILITIES		$		
WASTE DISPOSAL		$		
TOTAL OPERATING EXPENSE		$		
NET ORDINARY INCOME		$		
OTHER INCOME		$		
OTHER EXPENSES		$		
NET INCOME		$		

BUSINESS NAME

PROFIT AND LOSS STATEMENT – DATE: TO			
	REVENUES			
	$		$
	$		$
	$		$
	$		$
	$		$
TOTAL REVENUES		$	
COST OF GOODS SOLD		$	
GROSS PROFIT		$	
	OPERATING EXPENSES			
ADVERTISING		$	
AMORTIZATION		$	
AUTOMOBILE EXPENSES		$	
CHARITABLE CONTRIBUTIONS		$	
DEPRECIATION		$	
EQUIPMENT RENTAL		$	
INSURANCE		$	
INTEREST EXPENSE		$	
LICENSES		$	
OFFICE SUPPLIES		$	
OFFICER COMPENSATION		$	
PAYROLL EXPENSES		$	
RENT		$	
TELEPHONE		$	
TRAVEL & ENTERTAINMENT		$	
UTILITIES		$	
WASTE DISPOSAL		$	
TOTAL OPERATING EXPENSE		$	
NET ORDINARY INCOME		$	
OTHER INCOME		$	
OTHER EXPENSES		$	
NET INCOME		$	

BUSINESS NAME

PROFIT AND LOSS STATEMENT − DATE: TO				
\multicolumn{5}{c}{REVENUES}				
	$			$
	$			$
	$			$
	$			$
	$			$
TOTAL REVENUES	$			
COST OF GOODS SOLD	$			
GROSS PROFIT	$			
\multicolumn{5}{c}{OPERATING EXPENSES}				
ADVERTISING	$			
AMORTIZATION	$			
AUTOMOBILE EXPENSES	$			
CHARITABLE CONTRIBUTIONS	$			
DEPRECIATION	$			
EQUIPMENT RENTAL	$			
INSURANCE	$			
INTEREST EXPENSE	$			
LICENSES	$			
OFFICE SUPPLIES	$			
OFFICER COMPENSATION	$			
PAYROLL EXPENSES	$			
RENT	$			
TELEPHONE	$			
TRAVEL & ENTERTAINMENT	$			
UTILITIES	$			
WASTE DISPOSAL	$			
TOTAL OPERATING EXPENSE	$			
NET ORDINARY INCOME	$			
OTHER INCOME	$			
OTHER EXPENSES	$			
NET INCOME	$			

BUSINESS NAME

PROFIT AND LOSS STATEMENT – DATE: TO			
REVENUES			
	$		$
	$		$
	$		$
	$		$
	$		$
TOTAL REVENUES	$		
COST OF GOODS SOLD	$		
GROSS PROFIT	$		
OPERATING EXPENSES			
ADVERTISING	$		
AMORTIZATION	$		
AUTOMOBILE EXPENSES	$		
CHARITABLE CONTRIBUTIONS	$		
DEPRECIATION	$		
EQUIPMENT RENTAL	$		
INSURANCE	$		
INTEREST EXPENSE	$		
LICENSES	$		
OFFICE SUPPLIES	$		
OFFICER COMPENSATION	$		
PAYROLL EXPENSES	$		
RENT	$		
TELEPHONE	$		
TRAVEL & ENTERTAINMENT	$		
UTILITIES	$		
WASTE DISPOSAL	$		
TOTAL OPERATING EXPENSE	$		
NET ORDINARY INCOME	$		
OTHER INCOME	$		
OTHER EXPENSES	$		
NET INCOME	$		

BUSINESS NAME

PROFIT AND LOSS STATEMENT − DATE: TO				
	REVENUES				
	$			$
	$			$
	$			$
	$			$
	$			$
TOTAL REVENUES		$		
COST OF GOODS SOLD		$		
GROSS PROFIT		$		
	OPERATING EXPENSES				
ADVERTISING		$		
AMORTIZATION		$		
AUTOMOBILE EXPENSES		$		
CHARITABLE CONTRIBUTIONS		$		
DEPRECIATION		$		
EQUIPMENT RENTAL		$		
INSURANCE		$		
INTEREST EXPENSE		$		
LICENSES		$		
OFFICE SUPPLIES		$		
OFFICER COMPENSATION		$		
PAYROLL EXPENSES		$		
RENT		$		
TELEPHONE		$		
TRAVEL & ENTERTAINMENT		$		
UTILITIES		$		
WASTE DISPOSAL		$		
TOTAL OPERATING EXPENSE		$		
NET ORDINARY INCOME		$		
OTHER INCOME		$		
OTHER EXPENSES		$		
NET INCOME		$		

BUSINESS NAME

PROFIT AND LOSS STATEMENT – DATE: TO			
REVENUES			
	$		$
	$		$
	$		$
	$		$
	$		$
TOTAL REVENUES	$		
COST OF GOODS SOLD	$		
GROSS PROFIT	$		
OPERATING EXPENSES			
ADVERTISING	$		
AMORTIZATION	$		
AUTOMOBILE EXPENSES	$		
CHARITABLE CONTRIBUTIONS	$		
DEPRECIATION	$		
EQUIPMENT RENTAL	$		
INSURANCE	$		
INTEREST EXPENSE	$		
LICENSES	$		
OFFICE SUPPLIES	$		
OFFICER COMPENSATION	$		
PAYROLL EXPENSES	$		
RENT	$		
TELEPHONE	$		
TRAVEL & ENTERTAINMENT	$		
UTILITIES	$		
WASTE DISPOSAL	$		
TOTAL OPERATING EXPENSE	$		
NET ORDINARY INCOME	$		
OTHER INCOME	$		
OTHER EXPENSES	$		
NET INCOME	$		

BUSINESS NAME

PROFIT AND LOSS STATEMENT – DATE: TO				
REVENUES			
	$		$
	$		$
	$		$
	$		$
	$		$
TOTAL REVENUES	$		
COST OF GOODS SOLD	$		
GROSS PROFIT	$		
OPERATING EXPENSES			
ADVERTISING	$		
AMORTIZATION	$		
AUTOMOBILE EXPENSES	$		
CHARITABLE CONTRIBUTIONS	$		
DEPRECIATION	$		
EQUIPMENT RENTAL	$		
INSURANCE	$		
INTEREST EXPENSE	$		
LICENSES	$		
OFFICE SUPPLIES	$		
OFFICER COMPENSATION	$		
PAYROLL EXPENSES	$		
RENT	$		
TELEPHONE	$		
TRAVEL & ENTERTAINMENT	$		
UTILITIES	$		
WASTE DISPOSAL	$		
TOTAL OPERATING EXPENSE	$		
NET ORDINARY INCOME	$		
OTHER INCOME	$		
OTHER EXPENSES	$		
NET INCOME	$		

BUSINESS NAME

PROFIT AND LOSS STATEMENT — DATE: TO				
REVENUES				
	$			$
	$			$
	$			$
	$			$
	$			$
TOTAL REVENUES		$		
COST OF GOODS SOLD		$		
GROSS PROFIT		$		
OPERATING EXPENSES				
ADVERTISING		$		
AMORTIZATION		$		
AUTOMOBILE EXPENSES		$		
CHARITABLE CONTRIBUTIONS		$		
DEPRECIATION		$		
EQUIPMENT RENTAL		$		
INSURANCE		$		
INTEREST EXPENSE		$		
LICENSES		$		
OFFICE SUPPLIES		$		
OFFICER COMPENSATION		$		
PAYROLL EXPENSES		$		
RENT		$		
TELEPHONE		$		
TRAVEL & ENTERTAINMENT		$		
UTILITIES		$		
WASTE DISPOSAL		$		
TOTAL OPERATING EXPENSE		$		
NET ORDINARY INCOME		$		
OTHER INCOME		$		
OTHER EXPENSES		$		
NET INCOME		$		

BUSINESS NAME

PROFIT AND LOSS STATEMENT – DATE: TO			
REVENUES			
	$		$
	$		$
	$		$
	$		$
	$		$
TOTAL REVENUES		$	
COST OF GOODS SOLD		$	
GROSS PROFIT		$	
OPERATING EXPENSES			
ADVERTISING		$	
AMORTIZATION		$	
AUTOMOBILE EXPENSES		$	
CHARITABLE CONTRIBUTIONS		$	
DEPRECIATION		$	
EQUIPMENT RENTAL		$	
INSURANCE		$	
INTEREST EXPENSE		$	
LICENSES		$	
OFFICE SUPPLIES		$	
OFFICER COMPENSATION		$	
PAYROLL EXPENSES		$	
RENT		$	
TELEPHONE		$	
TRAVEL & ENTERTAINMENT		$	
UTILITIES		$	
WASTE DISPOSAL		$	
TOTAL OPERATING EXPENSE		$	
NET ORDINARY INCOME		$	
OTHER INCOME		$	
OTHER EXPENSES		$	
NET INCOME		$	

BUSINESS NAME

PROFIT AND LOSS STATEMENT – DATE: TO			
REVENUES			
	$		$
	$		$
	$		$
	$		$
	$		$
TOTAL REVENUES	$		
COST OF GOODS SOLD	$		
GROSS PROFIT	$		
OPERATING EXPENSES			
ADVERTISING	$		
AMORTIZATION	$		
AUTOMOBILE EXPENSES	$		
CHARITABLE CONTRIBUTIONS	$		
DEPRECIATION	$		
EQUIPMENT RENTAL	$		
INSURANCE	$		
INTEREST EXPENSE	$		
LICENSES	$		
OFFICE SUPPLIES	$		
OFFICER COMPENSATION	$		
PAYROLL EXPENSES	$		
RENT	$		
TELEPHONE	$		
TRAVEL & ENTERTAINMENT	$		
UTILITIES	$		
WASTE DISPOSAL	$		
TOTAL OPERATING EXPENSE	$		
NET ORDINARY INCOME	$		
OTHER INCOME	$		
OTHER EXPENSES	$		
NET INCOME	$		

BUSINESS NAME

PROFIT AND LOSS STATEMENT - DATE: TO			
REVENUES			
	$		$
	$		$
	$		$
	$		$
	$		$
TOTAL REVENUES	$		
COST OF GOODS SOLD	$		
GROSS PROFIT	$		
OPERATING EXPENSES			
ADVERTISING	$		
AMORTIZATION	$		
AUTOMOBILE EXPENSES	$		
CHARITABLE CONTRIBUTIONS	$		
DEPRECIATION	$		
EQUIPMENT RENTAL	$		
INSURANCE	$		
INTEREST EXPENSE	$		
LICENSES	$		
OFFICE SUPPLIES	$		
OFFICER COMPENSATION	$		
PAYROLL EXPENSES	$		
RENT	$		
TELEPHONE	$		
TRAVEL & ENTERTAINMENT	$		
UTILITIES	$		
WASTE DISPOSAL	$		
TOTAL OPERATING EXPENSE	$		
NET ORDINARY INCOME	$		
OTHER INCOME	$		
OTHER EXPENSES	$		
NET INCOME	$		

BUSINESS NAME

PROFIT AND LOSS STATEMENT - DATE:		TO	
\multicolumn{4}{c}{REVENUES}			
	$		$
	$		$
	$		$
	$		$
	$		$
TOTAL REVENUES	$		
COST OF GOODS SOLD	$		
GROSS PROFIT	$		
\multicolumn{4}{c}{OPERATING EXPENSES}			
ADVERTISING	$		
AMORTIZATION	$		
AUTOMOBILE EXPENSES	$		
CHARITABLE CONTRIBUTIONS	$		
DEPRECIATION	$		
EQUIPMENT RENTAL	$		
INSURANCE	$		
INTEREST EXPENSE	$		
LICENSES	$		
OFFICE SUPPLIES	$		
OFFICER COMPENSATION	$		
PAYROLL EXPENSES	$		
RENT	$		
TELEPHONE	$		
TRAVEL & ENTERTAINMENT	$		
UTILITIES	$		
WASTE DISPOSAL	$		
TOTAL OPERATING EXPENSE	$		
NET ORDINARY INCOME	$		
OTHER INCOME	$		
OTHER EXPENSES	$		
NET INCOME	$		

BUSINESS NAME

PROFIT AND LOSS STATEMENT – DATE: TO				
REVENUES				
	$			$
	$			$
	$			$
	$			$
	$			$
TOTAL REVENUES	$			
COST OF GOODS SOLD	$			
GROSS PROFIT	$			
OPERATING EXPENSES				
ADVERTISING	$			
AMORTIZATION	$			
AUTOMOBILE EXPENSES	$			
CHARITABLE CONTRIBUTIONS	$			
DEPRECIATION	$			
EQUIPMENT RENTAL	$			
INSURANCE	$			
INTEREST EXPENSE	$			
LICENSES	$			
OFFICE SUPPLIES	$			
OFFICER COMPENSATION	$			
PAYROLL EXPENSES	$			
RENT	$			
TELEPHONE	$			
TRAVEL & ENTERTAINMENT	$			
UTILITIES	$			
WASTE DISPOSAL	$			
TOTAL OPERATING EXPENSE	$			
NET ORDINARY INCOME	$			
OTHER INCOME	$			
OTHER EXPENSES	$			
NET INCOME	$			

BUSINESS NAME

PROFIT AND LOSS STATEMENT – DATE: TO			
REVENUES			
	$		$
	$		$
	$		$
	$		$
	$		$
TOTAL REVENUES		$	
COST OF GOODS SOLD		$	
GROSS PROFIT		$	
OPERATING EXPENSES			
ADVERTISING		$	
AMORTIZATION		$	
AUTOMOBILE EXPENSES		$	
CHARITABLE CONTRIBUTIONS		$	
DEPRECIATION		$	
EQUIPMENT RENTAL		$	
INSURANCE		$	
INTEREST EXPENSE		$	
LICENSES		$	
OFFICE SUPPLIES		$	
OFFICER COMPENSATION		$	
PAYROLL EXPENSES		$	
RENT		$	
TELEPHONE		$	
TRAVEL & ENTERTAINMENT		$	
UTILITIES		$	
WASTE DISPOSAL		$	
TOTAL OPERATING EXPENSE		$	
NET ORDINARY INCOME		$	
OTHER INCOME		$	
OTHER EXPENSES		$	
NET INCOME		$	

BUSINESS NAME

PROFIT AND LOSS STATEMENT – DATE: TO				
	$			$
	$			$
	$			$
	$			$
	$			$
TOTAL REVENUES	$			
COST OF GOODS SOLD	$			
GROSS PROFIT	$			
OPERATING EXPENSES				
ADVERTISING	$			
AMORTIZATION	$			
AUTOMOBILE EXPENSES	$			
CHARITABLE CONTRIBUTIONS	$			
DEPRECIATION	$			
EQUIPMENT RENTAL	$			
INSURANCE	$			
INTEREST EXPENSE	$			
LICENSES	$			
OFFICE SUPPLIES	$			
OFFICER COMPENSATION	$			
PAYROLL EXPENSES	$			
RENT	$			
TELEPHONE	$			
TRAVEL & ENTERTAINMENT	$			
UTILITIES	$			
WASTE DISPOSAL	$			
TOTAL OPERATING EXPENSE	$			
NET ORDINARY INCOME	$			
OTHER INCOME	$			
OTHER EXPENSES	$			
NET INCOME	$			

BUSINESS NAME

PROFIT AND LOSS STATEMENT – DATE: TO			
REVENUES			
	$		$
	$		$
	$		$
	$		$
	$		$
TOTAL REVENUES	$		
COST OF GOODS SOLD	$		
GROSS PROFIT	$		
OPERATING EXPENSES			
ADVERTISING	$		
AMORTIZATION	$		
AUTOMOBILE EXPENSES	$		
CHARITABLE CONTRIBUTIONS	$		
DEPRECIATION	$		
EQUIPMENT RENTAL	$		
INSURANCE	$		
INTEREST EXPENSE	$		
LICENSES	$		
OFFICE SUPPLIES	$		
OFFICER COMPENSATION	$		
PAYROLL EXPENSES	$		
RENT	$		
TELEPHONE	$		
TRAVEL & ENTERTAINMENT	$		
UTILITIES	$		
WASTE DISPOSAL	$		
TOTAL OPERATING EXPENSE	$		
NET ORDINARY INCOME	$		
OTHER INCOME	$		
OTHER EXPENSES	$		
NET INCOME	$		

BUSINESS NAME

PROFIT AND LOSS STATEMENT – DATE: TO			
	$		$
	$		$
	$		$
	$		$
	$		$
TOTAL REVENUES	$		
COST OF GOODS SOLD	$		
GROSS PROFIT	$		
OPERATING EXPENSES			
ADVERTISING	$		
AMORTIZATION	$		
AUTOMOBILE EXPENSES	$		
CHARITABLE CONTRIBUTIONS	$		
DEPRECIATION	$		
EQUIPMENT RENTAL	$		
INSURANCE	$		
INTEREST EXPENSE	$		
LICENSES	$		
OFFICE SUPPLIES	$		
OFFICER COMPENSATION	$		
PAYROLL EXPENSES	$		
RENT	$		
TELEPHONE	$		
TRAVEL & ENTERTAINMENT	$		
UTILITIES	$		
WASTE DISPOSAL	$		
TOTAL OPERATING EXPENSE	$		
NET ORDINARY INCOME	$		
OTHER INCOME	$		
OTHER EXPENSES	$		
NET INCOME	$		

BUSINESS NAME

PROFIT AND LOSS STATEMENT		– DATE:	TO
	$		$
	$		$
	$		$
	$		$
	$		$
TOTAL REVENUES	$		
COST OF GOODS SOLD	$		
GROSS PROFIT	$		
OPERATING EXPENSES			
ADVERTISING	$		
AMORTIZATION	$		
AUTOMOBILE EXPENSES	$		
CHARITABLE CONTRIBUTIONS	$		
DEPRECIATION	$		
EQUIPMENT RENTAL	$		
INSURANCE	$		
INTEREST EXPENSE	$		
LICENSES	$		
OFFICE SUPPLIES	$		
OFFICER COMPENSATION	$		
PAYROLL EXPENSES	$		
RENT	$		
TELEPHONE	$		
TRAVEL & ENTERTAINMENT	$		
UTILITIES	$		
WASTE DISPOSAL	$		
TOTAL OPERATING EXPENSE	$		
NET ORDINARY INCOME	$		
OTHER INCOME	$		
OTHER EXPENSES	$		
NET INCOME	$		

BUSINESS NAME

PROFIT AND LOSS STATEMENT – DATE: TO			
	REVENUES		
	$		$
	$		$
	$		$
	$		$
	$		$
TOTAL REVENUES	$		
COST OF GOODS SOLD	$		
GROSS PROFIT	$		
OPERATING EXPENSES			
ADVERTISING	$		
AMORTIZATION	$		
AUTOMOBILE EXPENSES	$		
CHARITABLE CONTRIBUTIONS	$		
DEPRECIATION	$		
EQUIPMENT RENTAL	$		
INSURANCE	$		
INTEREST EXPENSE	$		
LICENSES	$		
OFFICE SUPPLIES	$		
OFFICER COMPENSATION	$		
PAYROLL EXPENSES	$		
RENT	$		
TELEPHONE	$		
TRAVEL & ENTERTAINMENT	$		
UTILITIES	$		
WASTE DISPOSAL	$		
TOTAL OPERATING EXPENSE	$		
NET ORDINARY INCOME	$		
OTHER INCOME	$		
OTHER EXPENSES	$		
NET INCOME	$		

BUSINESS NAME

PROFIT AND LOSS STATEMENT - DATE: TO				
REVENUES				
	$		$	
	$		$	
	$		$	
	$		$	
	$		$	
TOTAL REVENUES	$			
COST OF GOODS SOLD	$			
GROSS PROFIT	$			
OPERATING EXPENSES				
ADVERTISING	$			
AMORTIZATION	$			
AUTOMOBILE EXPENSES	$			
CHARITABLE CONTRIBUTIONS	$			
DEPRECIATION	$			
EQUIPMENT RENTAL	$			
INSURANCE	$			
INTEREST EXPENSE	$			
LICENSES	$			
OFFICE SUPPLIES	$			
OFFICER COMPENSATION	$			
PAYROLL EXPENSES	$			
RENT	$			
TELEPHONE	$			
TRAVEL & ENTERTAINMENT	$			
UTILITIES	$			
WASTE DISPOSAL	$			
TOTAL OPERATING EXPENSE	$			
NET ORDINARY INCOME	$			
OTHER INCOME	$			
OTHER EXPENSES	$			
NET INCOME	$			

BUSINESS NAME

PROFIT AND LOSS STATEMENT – DATE: TO			
REVENUES			
	$		$
	$		$
	$		$
	$		$
	$		$
TOTAL REVENUES	$		
COST OF GOODS SOLD	$		
GROSS PROFIT	$		
OPERATING EXPENSES			
ADVERTISING	$		
AMORTIZATION	$		
AUTOMOBILE EXPENSES	$		
CHARITABLE CONTRIBUTIONS	$		
DEPRECIATION	$		
EQUIPMENT RENTAL	$		
INSURANCE	$		
INTEREST EXPENSE	$		
LICENSES	$		
OFFICE SUPPLIES	$		
OFFICER COMPENSATION	$		
PAYROLL EXPENSES	$		
RENT	$		
TELEPHONE	$		
TRAVEL & ENTERTAINMENT	$		
UTILITIES	$		
WASTE DISPOSAL	$		
TOTAL OPERATING EXPENSE	$		
NET ORDINARY INCOME	$		
OTHER INCOME	$		
OTHER EXPENSES	$		
NET INCOME	$		

BUSINESS NAME

PROFIT AND LOSS STATEMENT - DATE: TO			
	$		$
	$		$
	$		$
	$		$
	$		$
TOTAL REVENUES	$		
COST OF GOODS SOLD	$		
GROSS PROFIT	$		
OPERATING EXPENSES			
ADVERTISING	$		
AMORTIZATION	$		
AUTOMOBILE EXPENSES	$		
CHARITABLE CONTRIBUTIONS	$		
DEPRECIATION	$		
EQUIPMENT RENTAL	$		
INSURANCE	$		
INTEREST EXPENSE	$		
LICENSES	$		
OFFICE SUPPLIES	$		
OFFICER COMPENSATION	$		
PAYROLL EXPENSES	$		
RENT	$		
TELEPHONE	$		
TRAVEL & ENTERTAINMENT	$		
UTILITIES	$		
WASTE DISPOSAL	$		
TOTAL OPERATING EXPENSE	$		
NET ORDINARY INCOME	$		
OTHER INCOME	$		
OTHER EXPENSES	$		
NET INCOME	$		

BUSINESS NAME

PROFIT AND LOSS STATEMENT – DATE: TO				
	$			$
	$			$
	$			$
	$			$
	$			$
TOTAL REVENUES		$		
COST OF GOODS SOLD		$		
GROSS PROFIT		$		
OPERATING EXPENSES				
ADVERTISING		$		
AMORTIZATION		$		
AUTOMOBILE EXPENSES		$		
CHARITABLE CONTRIBUTIONS		$		
DEPRECIATION		$		
EQUIPMENT RENTAL		$		
INSURANCE		$		
INTEREST EXPENSE		$		
LICENSES		$		
OFFICE SUPPLIES		$		
OFFICER COMPENSATION		$		
PAYROLL EXPENSES		$		
RENT		$		
TELEPHONE		$		
TRAVEL & ENTERTAINMENT		$		
UTILITIES		$		
WASTE DISPOSAL		$		
TOTAL OPERATING EXPENSE		$		
NET ORDINARY INCOME		$		
OTHER INCOME		$		
OTHER EXPENSES		$		
NET INCOME		$		

BUSINESS NAME

PROFIT AND LOSS STATEMENT – DATE: TO			
	$		$
	$		$
	$		$
	$		$
	$		$
TOTAL REVENUES	$		
COST OF GOODS SOLD	$		
GROSS PROFIT	$		
OPERATING EXPENSES			
ADVERTISING	$		
AMORTIZATION	$		
AUTOMOBILE EXPENSES	$		
CHARITABLE CONTRIBUTIONS	$		
DEPRECIATION	$		
EQUIPMENT RENTAL	$		
INSURANCE	$		
INTEREST EXPENSE	$		
LICENSES	$		
OFFICE SUPPLIES	$		
OFFICER COMPENSATION	$		
PAYROLL EXPENSES	$		
RENT	$		
TELEPHONE	$		
TRAVEL & ENTERTAINMENT	$		
UTILITIES	$		
WASTE DISPOSAL	$		
TOTAL OPERATING EXPENSE	$		
NET ORDINARY INCOME	$		
OTHER INCOME	$		
OTHER EXPENSES	$		
NET INCOME	$		

BUSINESS NAME

PROFIT AND LOSS STATEMENT - DATE: TO			
	$		$
	$		$
	$		$
	$		$
	$		$
TOTAL REVENUES	$		
COST OF GOODS SOLD	$		
GROSS PROFIT	$		
OPERATING EXPENSES			
ADVERTISING	$		
AMORTIZATION	$		
AUTOMOBILE EXPENSES	$		
CHARITABLE CONTRIBUTIONS	$		
DEPRECIATION	$		
EQUIPMENT RENTAL	$		
INSURANCE	$		
INTEREST EXPENSE	$		
LICENSES	$		
OFFICE SUPPLIES	$		
OFFICER COMPENSATION	$		
PAYROLL EXPENSES	$		
RENT	$		
TELEPHONE	$		
TRAVEL & ENTERTAINMENT	$		
UTILITIES	$		
WASTE DISPOSAL	$		
TOTAL OPERATING EXPENSE	$		
NET ORDINARY INCOME	$		
OTHER INCOME	$		
OTHER EXPENSES	$		
NET INCOME	$		

BUSINESS NAME

PROFIT AND LOSS STATEMENT – DATE: TO				
REVENUES				
	$			$
	$			$
	$			$
	$			$
	$			$
TOTAL REVENUES	$			
COST OF GOODS SOLD	$			
GROSS PROFIT	$			
OPERATING EXPENSES				
ADVERTISING	$			
AMORTIZATION	$			
AUTOMOBILE EXPENSES	$			
CHARITABLE CONTRIBUTIONS	$			
DEPRECIATION	$			
EQUIPMENT RENTAL	$			
INSURANCE	$			
INTEREST EXPENSE	$			
LICENSES	$			
OFFICE SUPPLIES	$			
OFFICER COMPENSATION	$			
PAYROLL EXPENSES	$			
RENT	$			
TELEPHONE	$			
TRAVEL & ENTERTAINMENT	$			
UTILITIES	$			
WASTE DISPOSAL	$			
TOTAL OPERATING EXPENSE	$			
NET ORDINARY INCOME	$			
OTHER INCOME	$			
OTHER EXPENSES	$			
NET INCOME	$			

BUSINESS NAME

PROFIT AND LOSS STATEMENT – DATE: TO			
	$		$
	$		$
	$		$
	$		$
	$		$
TOTAL REVENUES	$		
COST OF GOODS SOLD	$		
GROSS PROFIT	$		
OPERATING EXPENSES			
ADVERTISING	$		
AMORTIZATION	$		
AUTOMOBILE EXPENSES	$		
CHARITABLE CONTRIBUTIONS	$		
DEPRECIATION	$		
EQUIPMENT RENTAL	$		
INSURANCE	$		
INTEREST EXPENSE	$		
LICENSES	$		
OFFICE SUPPLIES	$		
OFFICER COMPENSATION	$		
PAYROLL EXPENSES	$		
RENT	$		
TELEPHONE	$		
TRAVEL & ENTERTAINMENT	$		
UTILITIES	$		
WASTE DISPOSAL	$		
TOTAL OPERATING EXPENSE	$		
NET ORDINARY INCOME	$		
OTHER INCOME	$		
OTHER EXPENSES	$		
NET INCOME	$		

BUSINESS NAME

PROFIT AND LOSS STATEMENT		– DATE:	TO
	$		$
	$		$
	$		$
	$		$
	$		$
TOTAL REVENUES		$	
COST OF GOODS SOLD		$	
GROSS PROFIT		$	
OPERATING EXPENSES			
ADVERTISING		$	
AMORTIZATION		$	
AUTOMOBILE EXPENSES		$	
CHARITABLE CONTRIBUTIONS		$	
DEPRECIATION		$	
EQUIPMENT RENTAL		$	
INSURANCE		$	
INTEREST EXPENSE		$	
LICENSES		$	
OFFICE SUPPLIES		$	
OFFICER COMPENSATION		$	
PAYROLL EXPENSES		$	
RENT		$	
TELEPHONE		$	
TRAVEL & ENTERTAINMENT		$	
UTILITIES		$	
WASTE DISPOSAL		$	
TOTAL OPERATING EXPENSE		$	
NET ORDINARY INCOME		$	
OTHER INCOME		$	
OTHER EXPENSES		$	
NET INCOME		$	

BUSINESS NAME

PROFIT AND LOSS STATEMENT – DATE: TO			
REVENUES			
	$		$
	$		$
	$		$
	$		$
	$		$
TOTAL REVENUES	$		
COST OF GOODS SOLD	$		
GROSS PROFIT	$		
OPERATING EXPENSES			
ADVERTISING	$		
AMORTIZATION	$		
AUTOMOBILE EXPENSES	$		
CHARITABLE CONTRIBUTIONS	$		
DEPRECIATION	$		
EQUIPMENT RENTAL	$		
INSURANCE	$		
INTEREST EXPENSE	$		
LICENSES	$		
OFFICE SUPPLIES	$		
OFFICER COMPENSATION	$		
PAYROLL EXPENSES	$		
RENT	$		
TELEPHONE	$		
TRAVEL & ENTERTAINMENT	$		
UTILITIES	$		
WASTE DISPOSAL	$		
TOTAL OPERATING EXPENSE	$		
NET ORDINARY INCOME	$		
OTHER INCOME	$		
OTHER EXPENSES	$		
NET INCOME	$		

BUSINESS NAME

PROFIT AND LOSS STATEMENT - DATE:			TO
\multicolumn{4}{c}{REVENUES}			
	$		$
	$		$
	$		$
	$		$
	$		$
TOTAL REVENUES		$	
COST OF GOODS SOLD		$	
GROSS PROFIT		$	
\multicolumn{4}{c}{OPERATING EXPENSES}			
ADVERTISING		$	
AMORTIZATION		$	
AUTOMOBILE EXPENSES		$	
CHARITABLE CONTRIBUTIONS		$	
DEPRECIATION		$	
EQUIPMENT RENTAL		$	
INSURANCE		$	
INTEREST EXPENSE		$	
LICENSES		$	
OFFICE SUPPLIES		$	
OFFICER COMPENSATION		$	
PAYROLL EXPENSES		$	
RENT		$	
TELEPHONE		$	
TRAVEL & ENTERTAINMENT		$	
UTILITIES		$	
WASTE DISPOSAL		$	
TOTAL OPERATING EXPENSE		$	
NET ORDINARY INCOME		$	
OTHER INCOME		$	
OTHER EXPENSES		$	
NET INCOME		$	

BUSINESS NAME

PROFIT AND LOSS STATEMENT - DATE: TO			
REVENUES			
	$		$
	$		$
	$		$
	$		$
	$		$
TOTAL REVENUES		$	
COST OF GOODS SOLD		$	
GROSS PROFIT		$	
OPERATING EXPENSES			
ADVERTISING		$	
AMORTIZATION		$	
AUTOMOBILE EXPENSES		$	
CHARITABLE CONTRIBUTIONS		$	
DEPRECIATION		$	
EQUIPMENT RENTAL		$	
INSURANCE		$	
INTEREST EXPENSE		$	
LICENSES		$	
OFFICE SUPPLIES		$	
OFFICER COMPENSATION		$	
PAYROLL EXPENSES		$	
RENT		$	
TELEPHONE		$	
TRAVEL & ENTERTAINMENT		$	
UTILITIES		$	
WASTE DISPOSAL		$	
TOTAL OPERATING EXPENSE		$	
NET ORDINARY INCOME		$	
OTHER INCOME		$	
OTHER EXPENSES		$	
NET INCOME		$	

BUSINESS NAME

PROFIT AND LOSS STATEMENT – DATE: TO			
	REVENUES			
	$		$
	$		$
	$		$
	$		$
	$		$
TOTAL REVENUES	$		
COST OF GOODS SOLD	$		
GROSS PROFIT	$		
	OPERATING EXPENSES			
ADVERTISING	$		
AMORTIZATION	$		
AUTOMOBILE EXPENSES	$		
CHARITABLE CONTRIBUTIONS	$		
DEPRECIATION	$		
EQUIPMENT RENTAL	$		
INSURANCE	$		
INTEREST EXPENSE	$		
LICENSES	$		
OFFICE SUPPLIES	$		
OFFICER COMPENSATION	$		
PAYROLL EXPENSES	$		
RENT	$		
TELEPHONE	$		
TRAVEL & ENTERTAINMENT	$		
UTILITIES	$		
WASTE DISPOSAL	$		
TOTAL OPERATING EXPENSE	$		
NET ORDINARY INCOME	$		
OTHER INCOME	$		
OTHER EXPENSES	$		
NET INCOME	$		

BUSINESS NAME

PROFIT AND LOSS STATEMENT – DATE: TO			
REVENUES			
	$		$
	$		$
	$		$
	$		$
	$		$
TOTAL REVENUES	$		
COST OF GOODS SOLD	$		
GROSS PROFIT	$		
OPERATING EXPENSES			
ADVERTISING	$		
AMORTIZATION	$		
AUTOMOBILE EXPENSES	$		
CHARITABLE CONTRIBUTIONS	$		
DEPRECIATION	$		
EQUIPMENT RENTAL	$		
INSURANCE	$		
INTEREST EXPENSE	$		
LICENSES	$		
OFFICE SUPPLIES	$		
OFFICER COMPENSATION	$		
PAYROLL EXPENSES	$		
RENT	$		
TELEPHONE	$		
TRAVEL & ENTERTAINMENT	$		
UTILITIES	$		
WASTE DISPOSAL	$		
TOTAL OPERATING EXPENSE	$		
NET ORDINARY INCOME	$		
OTHER INCOME	$		
OTHER EXPENSES	$		
NET INCOME	$		

BUSINESS NAME

PROFIT AND LOSS STATEMENT – DATE: TO				
\multicolumn{5}{|c|}{REVENUES}				
	$		$	
	$		$	
	$		$	
	$		$	
	$		$	
TOTAL REVENUES	$			
COST OF GOODS SOLD	$			
GROSS PROFIT	$			
\multicolumn{5}{|c|}{OPERATING EXPENSES}				
ADVERTISING	$			
AMORTIZATION	$			
AUTOMOBILE EXPENSES	$			
CHARITABLE CONTRIBUTIONS	$			
DEPRECIATION	$			
EQUIPMENT RENTAL	$			
INSURANCE	$			
INTEREST EXPENSE	$			
LICENSES	$			
OFFICE SUPPLIES	$			
OFFICER COMPENSATION	$			
PAYROLL EXPENSES	$			
RENT	$			
TELEPHONE	$			
TRAVEL & ENTERTAINMENT	$			
UTILITIES	$			
WASTE DISPOSAL	$			
TOTAL OPERATING EXPENSE	$			
NET ORDINARY INCOME	$			
OTHER INCOME	$			
OTHER EXPENSES	$			
NET INCOME	$			

BUSINESS NAME

PROFIT AND LOSS STATEMENT − DATE: TO			
REVENUES			
	$		$
	$		$
	$		$
	$		$
	$		$
TOTAL REVENUES	$		
COST OF GOODS SOLD	$		
GROSS PROFIT	$		
OPERATING EXPENSES			
ADVERTISING	$		
AMORTIZATION	$		
AUTOMOBILE EXPENSES	$		
CHARITABLE CONTRIBUTIONS	$		
DEPRECIATION	$		
EQUIPMENT RENTAL	$		
INSURANCE	$		
INTEREST EXPENSE	$		
LICENSES	$		
OFFICE SUPPLIES	$		
OFFICER COMPENSATION	$		
PAYROLL EXPENSES	$		
RENT	$		
TELEPHONE	$		
TRAVEL & ENTERTAINMENT	$		
UTILITIES	$		
WASTE DISPOSAL	$		
TOTAL OPERATING EXPENSE	$		
NET ORDINARY INCOME	$		
OTHER INCOME	$		
OTHER EXPENSES	$		
NET INCOME	$		

BUSINESS NAME

PROFIT AND LOSS STATEMENT – DATE: TO			
	REVENUES			
	$		$
	$		$
	$		$
	$		$
	$		$
TOTAL REVENUES		$	
COST OF GOODS SOLD		$	
GROSS PROFIT		$	
	OPERATING EXPENSES			
ADVERTISING		$	
AMORTIZATION		$	
AUTOMOBILE EXPENSES		$	
CHARITABLE CONTRIBUTIONS		$	
DEPRECIATION		$	
EQUIPMENT RENTAL		$	
INSURANCE		$	
INTEREST EXPENSE		$	
LICENSES		$	
OFFICE SUPPLIES		$	
OFFICER COMPENSATION		$	
PAYROLL EXPENSES		$	
RENT		$	
TELEPHONE		$	
TRAVEL & ENTERTAINMENT		$	
UTILITIES		$	
WASTE DISPOSAL		$	
TOTAL OPERATING EXPENSE		$	
NET ORDINARY INCOME		$	
OTHER INCOME		$	
OTHER EXPENSES		$	
NET INCOME		$	

BUSINESS NAME

PROFIT AND LOSS STATEMENT - DATE: TO			
REVENUES			
	$		$
	$		$
	$		$
	$		$
	$		$
TOTAL REVENUES		$	
COST OF GOODS SOLD		$	
GROSS PROFIT		$	

OPERATING EXPENSES	
ADVERTISING	$
AMORTIZATION	$
AUTOMOBILE EXPENSES	$
CHARITABLE CONTRIBUTIONS	$
DEPRECIATION	$
EQUIPMENT RENTAL	$
INSURANCE	$
INTEREST EXPENSE	$
LICENSES	$
OFFICE SUPPLIES	$
OFFICER COMPENSATION	$
PAYROLL EXPENSES	$
RENT	$
TELEPHONE	$
TRAVEL & ENTERTAINMENT	$
UTILITIES	$
WASTE DISPOSAL	$
TOTAL OPERATING EXPENSE	$
NET ORDINARY INCOME	$
OTHER INCOME	$
OTHER EXPENSES	$
NET INCOME	$

BUSINESS NAME

PROFIT AND LOSS STATEMENT		- DATE:	TO
REVENUES			
	$		$
	$		$
	$		$
	$		$
	$		$
TOTAL REVENUES		$	
COST OF GOODS SOLD		$	
GROSS PROFIT		$	
OPERATING EXPENSES			
ADVERTISING		$	
AMORTIZATION		$	
AUTOMOBILE EXPENSES		$	
CHARITABLE CONTRIBUTIONS		$	
DEPRECIATION		$	
EQUIPMENT RENTAL		$	
INSURANCE		$	
INTEREST EXPENSE		$	
LICENSES		$	
OFFICE SUPPLIES		$	
OFFICER COMPENSATION		$	
PAYROLL EXPENSES		$	
RENT		$	
TELEPHONE		$	
TRAVEL & ENTERTAINMENT		$	
UTILITIES		$	
WASTE DISPOSAL		$	
TOTAL OPERATING EXPENSE		$	
NET ORDINARY INCOME		$	
OTHER INCOME		$	
OTHER EXPENSES		$	
NET INCOME		$	

BUSINESS NAME

PROFIT AND LOSS STATEMENT — DATE: TO			
REVENUES			
	$		$
	$		$
	$		$
	$		$
	$		$
TOTAL REVENUES		$	
COST OF GOODS SOLD		$	
GROSS PROFIT		$	
OPERATING EXPENSES			
ADVERTISING		$	
AMORTIZATION		$	
AUTOMOBILE EXPENSES		$	
CHARITABLE CONTRIBUTIONS		$	
DEPRECIATION		$	
EQUIPMENT RENTAL		$	
INSURANCE		$	
INTEREST EXPENSE		$	
LICENSES		$	
OFFICE SUPPLIES		$	
OFFICER COMPENSATION		$	
PAYROLL EXPENSES		$	
RENT		$	
TELEPHONE		$	
TRAVEL & ENTERTAINMENT		$	
UTILITIES		$	
WASTE DISPOSAL		$	
TOTAL OPERATING EXPENSE		$	
NET ORDINARY INCOME		$	
OTHER INCOME		$	
OTHER EXPENSES		$	
NET INCOME		$	

BUSINESS NAME

PROFIT AND LOSS STATEMENT - DATE: TO			
	$		$
	$		$
	$		$
	$		$
	$		$
TOTAL REVENUES	$		
COST OF GOODS SOLD	$		
GROSS PROFIT	$		
OPERATING EXPENSES			
ADVERTISING	$		
AMORTIZATION	$		
AUTOMOBILE EXPENSES	$		
CHARITABLE CONTRIBUTIONS	$		
DEPRECIATION	$		
EQUIPMENT RENTAL	$		
INSURANCE	$		
INTEREST EXPENSE	$		
LICENSES	$		
OFFICE SUPPLIES	$		
OFFICER COMPENSATION	$		
PAYROLL EXPENSES	$		
RENT	$		
TELEPHONE	$		
TRAVEL & ENTERTAINMENT	$		
UTILITIES	$		
WASTE DISPOSAL	$		
TOTAL OPERATING EXPENSE	$		
NET ORDINARY INCOME	$		
OTHER INCOME	$		
OTHER EXPENSES	$		
NET INCOME	$		

BUSINESS NAME

PROFIT AND LOSS STATEMENT - DATE: TO			
REVENUES			
	$		$
	$		$
	$		$
	$		$
	$		$
TOTAL REVENUES		$	
COST OF GOODS SOLD		$	
GROSS PROFIT		$	
OPERATING EXPENSES			
ADVERTISING		$	
AMORTIZATION		$	
AUTOMOBILE EXPENSES		$	
CHARITABLE CONTRIBUTIONS		$	
DEPRECIATION		$	
EQUIPMENT RENTAL		$	
INSURANCE		$	
INTEREST EXPENSE		$	
LICENSES		$	
OFFICE SUPPLIES		$	
OFFICER COMPENSATION		$	
PAYROLL EXPENSES		$	
RENT		$	
TELEPHONE		$	
TRAVEL & ENTERTAINMENT		$	
UTILITIES		$	
WASTE DISPOSAL		$	
TOTAL OPERATING EXPENSE		$	
NET ORDINARY INCOME		$	
OTHER INCOME		$	
OTHER EXPENSES		$	
NET INCOME		$	

BUSINESS NAME

PROFIT AND LOSS STATEMENT – DATE: TO			
	REVENUES			
	$		$
	$		$
	$		$
	$		$
	$		$
TOTAL REVENUES	$		
COST OF GOODS SOLD	$		
GROSS PROFIT	$		
	OPERATING EXPENSES			
ADVERTISING	$		
AMORTIZATION	$		
AUTOMOBILE EXPENSES	$		
CHARITABLE CONTRIBUTIONS	$		
DEPRECIATION	$		
EQUIPMENT RENTAL	$		
INSURANCE	$		
INTEREST EXPENSE	$		
LICENSES	$		
OFFICE SUPPLIES	$		
OFFICER COMPENSATION	$		
PAYROLL EXPENSES	$		
RENT	$		
TELEPHONE	$		
TRAVEL & ENTERTAINMENT	$		
UTILITIES	$		
WASTE DISPOSAL	$		
TOTAL OPERATING EXPENSE	$		
NET ORDINARY INCOME	$		
OTHER INCOME	$		
OTHER EXPENSES	$		
NET INCOME	$		

BUSINESS NAME

PROFIT AND LOSS STATEMENT – DATE: TO			
	REVENUES		
	$		$
	$		$
	$		$
	$		$
	$		$
TOTAL REVENUES	$		
COST OF GOODS SOLD	$		
GROSS PROFIT	$		
OPERATING EXPENSES			
ADVERTISING	$		
AMORTIZATION	$		
AUTOMOBILE EXPENSES	$		
CHARITABLE CONTRIBUTIONS	$		
DEPRECIATION	$		
EQUIPMENT RENTAL	$		
INSURANCE	$		
INTEREST EXPENSE	$		
LICENSES	$		
OFFICE SUPPLIES	$		
OFFICER COMPENSATION	$		
PAYROLL EXPENSES	$		
RENT	$		
TELEPHONE	$		
TRAVEL & ENTERTAINMENT	$		
UTILITIES	$		
WASTE DISPOSAL	$		
TOTAL OPERATING EXPENSE	$		
NET ORDINARY INCOME	$		
OTHER INCOME	$		
OTHER EXPENSES	$		
NET INCOME	$		

BUSINESS NAME

PROFIT AND LOSS STATEMENT - DATE: TO			
REVENUES			
	$		$
	$		$
	$		$
	$		$
	$		$
TOTAL REVENUES		$	
COST OF GOODS SOLD		$	
GROSS PROFIT		$	
OPERATING EXPENSES			
ADVERTISING		$	
AMORTIZATION		$	
AUTOMOBILE EXPENSES		$	
CHARITABLE CONTRIBUTIONS		$	
DEPRECIATION		$	
EQUIPMENT RENTAL		$	
INSURANCE		$	
INTEREST EXPENSE		$	
LICENSES		$	
OFFICE SUPPLIES		$	
OFFICER COMPENSATION		$	
PAYROLL EXPENSES		$	
RENT		$	
TELEPHONE		$	
TRAVEL & ENTERTAINMENT		$	
UTILITIES		$	
WASTE DISPOSAL		$	
TOTAL OPERATING EXPENSE		$	
NET ORDINARY INCOME		$	
OTHER INCOME		$	
OTHER EXPENSES		$	
NET INCOME		$	

BUSINESS NAME

PROFIT AND LOSS STATEMENT – DATE: TO			
REVENUES			
	$		$
	$		$
	$		$
	$		$
	$		$
TOTAL REVENUES	$		
COST OF GOODS SOLD	$		
GROSS PROFIT	$		
OPERATING EXPENSES			
ADVERTISING	$		
AMORTIZATION	$		
AUTOMOBILE EXPENSES	$		
CHARITABLE CONTRIBUTIONS	$		
DEPRECIATION	$		
EQUIPMENT RENTAL	$		
INSURANCE	$		
INTEREST EXPENSE	$		
LICENSES	$		
OFFICE SUPPLIES	$		
OFFICER COMPENSATION	$		
PAYROLL EXPENSES	$		
RENT	$		
TELEPHONE	$		
TRAVEL & ENTERTAINMENT	$		
UTILITIES	$		
WASTE DISPOSAL	$		
TOTAL OPERATING EXPENSE	$		
NET ORDINARY INCOME	$		
OTHER INCOME	$		
OTHER EXPENSES	$		
NET INCOME	$		

BUSINESS NAME

PROFIT AND LOSS STATEMENT		– DATE:	TO
	$		$
	$		$
	$		$
	$		$
	$		$
TOTAL REVENUES		$	
COST OF GOODS SOLD		$	
GROSS PROFIT		$	
OPERATING EXPENSES			
ADVERTISING		$	
AMORTIZATION		$	
AUTOMOBILE EXPENSES		$	
CHARITABLE CONTRIBUTIONS		$	
DEPRECIATION		$	
EQUIPMENT RENTAL		$	
INSURANCE		$	
INTEREST EXPENSE		$	
LICENSES		$	
OFFICE SUPPLIES		$	
OFFICER COMPENSATION		$	
PAYROLL EXPENSES		$	
RENT		$	
TELEPHONE		$	
TRAVEL & ENTERTAINMENT		$	
UTILITIES		$	
WASTE DISPOSAL		$	
TOTAL OPERATING EXPENSE		$	
NET ORDINARY INCOME		$	
OTHER INCOME		$	
OTHER EXPENSES		$	
NET INCOME		$	

BUSINESS NAME

PROFIT AND LOSS STATEMENT – DATE: TO			
	$		$
	$		$
	$		$
	$		$
	$		$
TOTAL REVENUES	$		
COST OF GOODS SOLD	$		
GROSS PROFIT	$		
OPERATING EXPENSES			
ADVERTISING	$		
AMORTIZATION	$		
AUTOMOBILE EXPENSES	$		
CHARITABLE CONTRIBUTIONS	$		
DEPRECIATION	$		
EQUIPMENT RENTAL	$		
INSURANCE	$		
INTEREST EXPENSE	$		
LICENSES	$		
OFFICE SUPPLIES	$		
OFFICER COMPENSATION	$		
PAYROLL EXPENSES	$		
RENT	$		
TELEPHONE	$		
TRAVEL & ENTERTAINMENT	$		
UTILITIES	$		
WASTE DISPOSAL	$		
TOTAL OPERATING EXPENSE	$		
NET ORDINARY INCOME	$		
OTHER INCOME	$		
OTHER EXPENSES	$		
NET INCOME	$		

BUSINESS NAME

PROFIT AND LOSS STATEMENT – DATE: TO			
	$		$
	$		$
	$		$
	$		$
	$		$
TOTAL REVENUES	$		
COST OF GOODS SOLD	$		
GROSS PROFIT	$		
OPERATING EXPENSES			
ADVERTISING	$		
AMORTIZATION	$		
AUTOMOBILE EXPENSES	$		
CHARITABLE CONTRIBUTIONS	$		
DEPRECIATION	$		
EQUIPMENT RENTAL	$		
INSURANCE	$		
INTEREST EXPENSE	$		
LICENSES	$		
OFFICE SUPPLIES	$		
OFFICER COMPENSATION	$		
PAYROLL EXPENSES	$		
RENT	$		
TELEPHONE	$		
TRAVEL & ENTERTAINMENT	$		
UTILITIES	$		
WASTE DISPOSAL	$		
TOTAL OPERATING EXPENSE	$		
NET ORDINARY INCOME	$		
OTHER INCOME	$		
OTHER EXPENSES	$		
NET INCOME	$		

BUSINESS NAME

PROFIT AND LOSS STATEMENT – DATE: TO			
REVENUES			
	$		$
	$		$
	$		$
	$		$
	$		$
TOTAL REVENUES	$		
COST OF GOODS SOLD	$		
GROSS PROFIT	$		
OPERATING EXPENSES			
ADVERTISING	$		
AMORTIZATION	$		
AUTOMOBILE EXPENSES	$		
CHARITABLE CONTRIBUTIONS	$		
DEPRECIATION	$		
EQUIPMENT RENTAL	$		
INSURANCE	$		
INTEREST EXPENSE	$		
LICENSES	$		
OFFICE SUPPLIES	$		
OFFICER COMPENSATION	$		
PAYROLL EXPENSES	$		
RENT	$		
TELEPHONE	$		
TRAVEL & ENTERTAINMENT	$		
UTILITIES	$		
WASTE DISPOSAL	$		
TOTAL OPERATING EXPENSE	$		
NET ORDINARY INCOME	$		
OTHER INCOME	$		
OTHER EXPENSES	$		
NET INCOME	$		

BUSINESS NAME

PROFIT AND LOSS STATEMENT − DATE: TO				
	REVENUES				
	$		$	
	$		$	
	$		$	
	$		$	
	$		$	
TOTAL REVENUES	$			
COST OF GOODS SOLD	$			
GROSS PROFIT	$			
	OPERATING EXPENSES				
ADVERTISING	$			
AMORTIZATION	$			
AUTOMOBILE EXPENSES	$			
CHARITABLE CONTRIBUTIONS	$			
DEPRECIATION	$			
EQUIPMENT RENTAL	$			
INSURANCE	$			
INTEREST EXPENSE	$			
LICENSES	$			
OFFICE SUPPLIES	$			
OFFICER COMPENSATION	$			
PAYROLL EXPENSES	$			
RENT	$			
TELEPHONE	$			
TRAVEL & ENTERTAINMENT	$			
UTILITIES	$			
WASTE DISPOSAL	$			
TOTAL OPERATING EXPENSE	$			
NET ORDINARY INCOME	$			
OTHER INCOME	$			
OTHER EXPENSES	$			
NET INCOME	$			

BUSINESS NAME

PROFIT AND LOSS STATEMENT – DATE: TO			
REVENUES			
	$		$
	$		$
	$		$
	$		$
	$		$
TOTAL REVENUES	$		
COST OF GOODS SOLD	$		
GROSS PROFIT	$		
OPERATING EXPENSES			
ADVERTISING	$		
AMORTIZATION	$		
AUTOMOBILE EXPENSES	$		
CHARITABLE CONTRIBUTIONS	$		
DEPRECIATION	$		
EQUIPMENT RENTAL	$		
INSURANCE	$		
INTEREST EXPENSE	$		
LICENSES	$		
OFFICE SUPPLIES	$		
OFFICER COMPENSATION	$		
PAYROLL EXPENSES	$		
RENT	$		
TELEPHONE	$		
TRAVEL & ENTERTAINMENT	$		
UTILITIES	$		
WASTE DISPOSAL	$		
TOTAL OPERATING EXPENSE	$		
NET ORDINARY INCOME	$		
OTHER INCOME	$		
OTHER EXPENSES	$		
NET INCOME	$		

BUSINESS NAME

PROFIT AND LOSS STATEMENT – DATE: TO			
REVENUES			
	$		$
	$		$
	$		$
	$		$
	$		$
TOTAL REVENUES	$		
COST OF GOODS SOLD	$		
GROSS PROFIT	$		
OPERATING EXPENSES			
ADVERTISING	$		
AMORTIZATION	$		
AUTOMOBILE EXPENSES	$		
CHARITABLE CONTRIBUTIONS	$		
DEPRECIATION	$		
EQUIPMENT RENTAL	$		
INSURANCE	$		
INTEREST EXPENSE	$		
LICENSES	$		
OFFICE SUPPLIES	$		
OFFICER COMPENSATION	$		
PAYROLL EXPENSES	$		
RENT	$		
TELEPHONE	$		
TRAVEL & ENTERTAINMENT	$		
UTILITIES	$		
WASTE DISPOSAL	$		
TOTAL OPERATING EXPENSE	$		
NET ORDINARY INCOME	$		
OTHER INCOME	$		
OTHER EXPENSES	$		
NET INCOME	$		

BUSINESS NAME

PROFIT AND LOSS STATEMENT – DATE: TO			
REVENUES			
	$		$
	$		$
	$		$
	$		$
	$		$
TOTAL REVENUES	$		
COST OF GOODS SOLD	$		
GROSS PROFIT	$		
OPERATING EXPENSES			
ADVERTISING	$		
AMORTIZATION	$		
AUTOMOBILE EXPENSES	$		
CHARITABLE CONTRIBUTIONS	$		
DEPRECIATION	$		
EQUIPMENT RENTAL	$		
INSURANCE	$		
INTEREST EXPENSE	$		
LICENSES	$		
OFFICE SUPPLIES	$		
OFFICER COMPENSATION	$		
PAYROLL EXPENSES	$		
RENT	$		
TELEPHONE	$		
TRAVEL & ENTERTAINMENT	$		
UTILITIES	$		
WASTE DISPOSAL	$		
TOTAL OPERATING EXPENSE	$		
NET ORDINARY INCOME	$		
OTHER INCOME	$		
OTHER EXPENSES	$		
NET INCOME	$		

BUSINESS NAME

PROFIT AND LOSS STATEMENT – DATE:		TO	
REVENUES			
	$		$
	$		$
	$		$
	$		$
	$		$
TOTAL REVENUES		$	
COST OF GOODS SOLD		$	
GROSS PROFIT		$	
OPERATING EXPENSES			
ADVERTISING		$	
AMORTIZATION		$	
AUTOMOBILE EXPENSES		$	
CHARITABLE CONTRIBUTIONS		$	
DEPRECIATION		$	
EQUIPMENT RENTAL		$	
INSURANCE		$	
INTEREST EXPENSE		$	
LICENSES		$	
OFFICE SUPPLIES		$	
OFFICER COMPENSATION		$	
PAYROLL EXPENSES		$	
RENT		$	
TELEPHONE		$	
TRAVEL & ENTERTAINMENT		$	
UTILITIES		$	
WASTE DISPOSAL		$	
TOTAL OPERATING EXPENSE		$	
NET ORDINARY INCOME		$	
OTHER INCOME		$	
OTHER EXPENSES		$	
NET INCOME		$	

BUSINESS NAME

PROFIT AND LOSS STATEMENT – DATE: TO			
REVENUES			
	$		$
	$		$
	$		$
	$		$
	$		$
TOTAL REVENUES	$		
COST OF GOODS SOLD	$		
GROSS PROFIT	$		
OPERATING EXPENSES			
ADVERTISING	$		
AMORTIZATION	$		
AUTOMOBILE EXPENSES	$		
CHARITABLE CONTRIBUTIONS	$		
DEPRECIATION	$		
EQUIPMENT RENTAL	$		
INSURANCE	$		
INTEREST EXPENSE	$		
LICENSES	$		
OFFICE SUPPLIES	$		
OFFICER COMPENSATION	$		
PAYROLL EXPENSES	$		
RENT	$		
TELEPHONE	$		
TRAVEL & ENTERTAINMENT	$		
UTILITIES	$		
WASTE DISPOSAL	$		
TOTAL OPERATING EXPENSE	$		
NET ORDINARY INCOME	$		
OTHER INCOME	$		
OTHER EXPENSES	$		
NET INCOME	$		

BUSINESS NAME

PROFIT AND LOSS STATEMENT	–	DATE:	TO
REVENUES			

	$		$
	$		$
	$		$
	$		$
	$		$
TOTAL REVENUES		$	
COST OF GOODS SOLD		$	
GROSS PROFIT		$	
OPERATING EXPENSES			
ADVERTISING		$	
AMORTIZATION		$	
AUTOMOBILE EXPENSES		$	
CHARITABLE CONTRIBUTIONS		$	
DEPRECIATION		$	
EQUIPMENT RENTAL		$	
INSURANCE		$	
INTEREST EXPENSE		$	
LICENSES		$	
OFFICE SUPPLIES		$	
OFFICER COMPENSATION		$	
PAYROLL EXPENSES		$	
RENT		$	
TELEPHONE		$	
TRAVEL & ENTERTAINMENT		$	
UTILITIES		$	
WASTE DISPOSAL		$	
TOTAL OPERATING EXPENSE		$	
NET ORDINARY INCOME		$	
OTHER INCOME		$	
OTHER EXPENSES		$	
NET INCOME		$	

BUSINESS NAME

PROFIT AND LOSS STATEMENT − DATE:		TO	
\multicolumn{4}{c}{REVENUES}			
	$		$
	$		$
	$		$
	$		$
	$		$
TOTAL REVENUES	$		
COST OF GOODS SOLD	$		
GROSS PROFIT	$		
\multicolumn{4}{c}{OPERATING EXPENSES}			
ADVERTISING	$		
AMORTIZATION	$		
AUTOMOBILE EXPENSES	$		
CHARITABLE CONTRIBUTIONS	$		
DEPRECIATION	$		
EQUIPMENT RENTAL	$		
INSURANCE	$		
INTEREST EXPENSE	$		
LICENSES	$		
OFFICE SUPPLIES	$		
OFFICER COMPENSATION	$		
PAYROLL EXPENSES	$		
RENT	$		
TELEPHONE	$		
TRAVEL & ENTERTAINMENT	$		
UTILITIES	$		
WASTE DISPOSAL	$		
TOTAL OPERATING EXPENSE	$		
NET ORDINARY INCOME	$		
OTHER INCOME	$		
OTHER EXPENSES	$		
NET INCOME	$		

BUSINESS NAME

PROFIT AND LOSS STATEMENT – DATE: TO				
REVENUES				
	$		$	
	$		$	
	$		$	
	$		$	
	$		$	
TOTAL REVENUES	$			
COST OF GOODS SOLD	$			
GROSS PROFIT	$			
OPERATING EXPENSES				
ADVERTISING	$			
AMORTIZATION	$			
AUTOMOBILE EXPENSES	$			
CHARITABLE CONTRIBUTIONS	$			
DEPRECIATION	$			
EQUIPMENT RENTAL	$			
INSURANCE	$			
INTEREST EXPENSE	$			
LICENSES	$			
OFFICE SUPPLIES	$			
OFFICER COMPENSATION	$			
PAYROLL EXPENSES	$			
RENT	$			
TELEPHONE	$			
TRAVEL & ENTERTAINMENT	$			
UTILITIES	$			
WASTE DISPOSAL	$			
TOTAL OPERATING EXPENSE	$			
NET ORDINARY INCOME	$			
OTHER INCOME	$			
OTHER EXPENSES	$			
NET INCOME	$			

BUSINESS NAME

PROFIT AND LOSS STATEMENT – DATE: TO				
	$			$
	$			$
	$			$
	$			$
	$			$
TOTAL REVENUES		$		
COST OF GOODS SOLD		$		
GROSS PROFIT		$		
OPERATING EXPENSES				
ADVERTISING		$		
AMORTIZATION		$		
AUTOMOBILE EXPENSES		$		
CHARITABLE CONTRIBUTIONS		$		
DEPRECIATION		$		
EQUIPMENT RENTAL		$		
INSURANCE		$		
INTEREST EXPENSE		$		
LICENSES		$		
OFFICE SUPPLIES		$		
OFFICER COMPENSATION		$		
PAYROLL EXPENSES		$		
RENT		$		
TELEPHONE		$		
TRAVEL & ENTERTAINMENT		$		
UTILITIES		$		
WASTE DISPOSAL		$		
TOTAL OPERATING EXPENSE		$		
NET ORDINARY INCOME		$		
OTHER INCOME		$		
OTHER EXPENSES		$		
NET INCOME		$		

BUSINESS NAME

PROFIT AND LOSS STATEMENT - DATE:		TO	
REVENUES			
	$		$
	$		$
	$		$
	$		$
	$		$
TOTAL REVENUES		$	
COST OF GOODS SOLD		$	
GROSS PROFIT		$	
OPERATING EXPENSES			
ADVERTISING		$	
AMORTIZATION		$	
AUTOMOBILE EXPENSES		$	
CHARITABLE CONTRIBUTIONS		$	
DEPRECIATION		$	
EQUIPMENT RENTAL		$	
INSURANCE		$	
INTEREST EXPENSE		$	
LICENSES		$	
OFFICE SUPPLIES		$	
OFFICER COMPENSATION		$	
PAYROLL EXPENSES		$	
RENT		$	
TELEPHONE		$	
TRAVEL & ENTERTAINMENT		$	
UTILITIES		$	
WASTE DISPOSAL		$	
TOTAL OPERATING EXPENSE		$	
NET ORDINARY INCOME		$	
OTHER INCOME		$	
OTHER EXPENSES		$	
NET INCOME		$	

BUSINESS NAME

PROFIT AND LOSS STATEMENT – DATE: TO			
REVENUES			
	$		$
	$		$
	$		$
	$		$
	$		$
TOTAL REVENUES	$		
COST OF GOODS SOLD	$		
GROSS PROFIT	$		
OPERATING EXPENSES			
ADVERTISING	$		
AMORTIZATION	$		
AUTOMOBILE EXPENSES	$		
CHARITABLE CONTRIBUTIONS	$		
DEPRECIATION	$		
EQUIPMENT RENTAL	$		
INSURANCE	$		
INTEREST EXPENSE	$		
LICENSES	$		
OFFICE SUPPLIES	$		
OFFICER COMPENSATION	$		
PAYROLL EXPENSES	$		
RENT	$		
TELEPHONE	$		
TRAVEL & ENTERTAINMENT	$		
UTILITIES	$		
WASTE DISPOSAL	$		
TOTAL OPERATING EXPENSE	$		
NET ORDINARY INCOME	$		
OTHER INCOME	$		
OTHER EXPENSES	$		
NET INCOME	$		

BUSINESS NAME

PROFIT AND LOSS STATEMENT – DATE: TO			
	REVENUES			
	$		$
	$		$
	$		$
	$		$
	$		$
TOTAL REVENUES	$		
COST OF GOODS SOLD	$		
GROSS PROFIT	$		
	OPERATING EXPENSES			
ADVERTISING	$		
AMORTIZATION	$		
AUTOMOBILE EXPENSES	$		
CHARITABLE CONTRIBUTIONS	$		
DEPRECIATION	$		
EQUIPMENT RENTAL	$		
INSURANCE	$		
INTEREST EXPENSE	$		
LICENSES	$		
OFFICE SUPPLIES	$		
OFFICER COMPENSATION	$		
PAYROLL EXPENSES	$		
RENT	$		
TELEPHONE	$		
TRAVEL & ENTERTAINMENT	$		
UTILITIES	$		
WASTE DISPOSAL	$		
TOTAL OPERATING EXPENSE	$		
NET ORDINARY INCOME	$		
OTHER INCOME	$		
OTHER EXPENSES	$		
NET INCOME	$		

BUSINESS NAME

PROFIT AND LOSS STATEMENT – DATE: TO			
REVENUES			
	$		$
	$		$
	$		$
	$		$
	$		$
TOTAL REVENUES	$		
COST OF GOODS SOLD	$		
GROSS PROFIT	$		
OPERATING EXPENSES			
ADVERTISING	$		
AMORTIZATION	$		
AUTOMOBILE EXPENSES	$		
CHARITABLE CONTRIBUTIONS	$		
DEPRECIATION	$		
EQUIPMENT RENTAL	$		
INSURANCE	$		
INTEREST EXPENSE	$		
LICENSES	$		
OFFICE SUPPLIES	$		
OFFICER COMPENSATION	$		
PAYROLL EXPENSES	$		
RENT	$		
TELEPHONE	$		
TRAVEL & ENTERTAINMENT	$		
UTILITIES	$		
WASTE DISPOSAL	$		
TOTAL OPERATING EXPENSE	$		
NET ORDINARY INCOME	$		
OTHER INCOME	$		
OTHER EXPENSES	$		
NET INCOME	$		

BUSINESS NAME

PROFIT AND LOSS STATEMENT − DATE: TO			
<td colspan="4" align="center">**REVENUES**</td>			
	$		$
	$		$
	$		$
	$		$
	$		$
TOTAL REVENUES	$		
COST OF GOODS SOLD	$		
GROSS PROFIT	$		
<td colspan="4" align="center">**OPERATING EXPENSES**</td>			
ADVERTISING	$		
AMORTIZATION	$		
AUTOMOBILE EXPENSES	$		
CHARITABLE CONTRIBUTIONS	$		
DEPRECIATION	$		
EQUIPMENT RENTAL	$		
INSURANCE	$		
INTEREST EXPENSE	$		
LICENSES	$		
OFFICE SUPPLIES	$		
OFFICER COMPENSATION	$		
PAYROLL EXPENSES	$		
RENT	$		
TELEPHONE	$		
TRAVEL & ENTERTAINMENT	$		
UTILITIES	$		
WASTE DISPOSAL	$		
TOTAL OPERATING EXPENSE	$		
NET ORDINARY INCOME	$		
OTHER INCOME	$		
OTHER EXPENSES	$		
NET INCOME	$		

BUSINESS NAME

PROFIT AND LOSS STATEMENT – DATE: TO				
	REVENUES				
	$			$
	$			$
	$			$
	$			$
	$			$
TOTAL REVENUES		$		
COST OF GOODS SOLD		$		
GROSS PROFIT		$		
	OPERATING EXPENSES				
ADVERTISING		$		
AMORTIZATION		$		
AUTOMOBILE EXPENSES		$		
CHARITABLE CONTRIBUTIONS		$		
DEPRECIATION		$		
EQUIPMENT RENTAL		$		
INSURANCE		$		
INTEREST EXPENSE		$		
LICENSES		$		
OFFICE SUPPLIES		$		
OFFICER COMPENSATION		$		
PAYROLL EXPENSES		$		
RENT		$		
TELEPHONE		$		
TRAVEL & ENTERTAINMENT		$		
UTILITIES		$		
WASTE DISPOSAL		$		
TOTAL OPERATING EXPENSE		$		
NET ORDINARY INCOME		$		
OTHER INCOME		$		
OTHER EXPENSES		$		
NET INCOME		$		

BUSINESS NAME

PROFIT AND LOSS STATEMENT – DATE:		TO	
\multicolumn{4}{c}{REVENUES}			
	$		$
	$		$
	$		$
	$		$
	$		$
TOTAL REVENUES	$		
COST OF GOODS SOLD	$		
GROSS PROFIT	$		
OPERATING EXPENSES			
ADVERTISING	$		
AMORTIZATION	$		
AUTOMOBILE EXPENSES	$		
CHARITABLE CONTRIBUTIONS	$		
DEPRECIATION	$		
EQUIPMENT RENTAL	$		
INSURANCE	$		
INTEREST EXPENSE	$		
LICENSES	$		
OFFICE SUPPLIES	$		
OFFICER COMPENSATION	$		
PAYROLL EXPENSES	$		
RENT	$		
TELEPHONE	$		
TRAVEL & ENTERTAINMENT	$		
UTILITIES	$		
WASTE DISPOSAL	$		
TOTAL OPERATING EXPENSE	$		
NET ORDINARY INCOME	$		
OTHER INCOME	$		
OTHER EXPENSES	$		
NET INCOME	$		

BUSINESS NAME

PROFIT AND LOSS STATEMENT – DATE: TO			
	$		$
	$		$
	$		$
	$		$
	$		$
TOTAL REVENUES	$		
COST OF GOODS SOLD	$		
GROSS PROFIT	$		
OPERATING EXPENSES			
ADVERTISING	$		
AMORTIZATION	$		
AUTOMOBILE EXPENSES	$		
CHARITABLE CONTRIBUTIONS	$		
DEPRECIATION	$		
EQUIPMENT RENTAL	$		
INSURANCE	$		
INTEREST EXPENSE	$		
LICENSES	$		
OFFICE SUPPLIES	$		
OFFICER COMPENSATION	$		
PAYROLL EXPENSES	$		
RENT	$		
TELEPHONE	$		
TRAVEL & ENTERTAINMENT	$		
UTILITIES	$		
WASTE DISPOSAL	$		
TOTAL OPERATING EXPENSE	$		
NET ORDINARY INCOME	$		
OTHER INCOME	$		
OTHER EXPENSES	$		
NET INCOME	$		

BUSINESS NAME

PROFIT AND LOSS STATEMENT - DATE:		TO	
REVENUES			
	$		$
	$		$
	$		$
	$		$
	$		$
TOTAL REVENUES		$	
COST OF GOODS SOLD		$	
GROSS PROFIT		$	
OPERATING EXPENSES			
ADVERTISING		$	
AMORTIZATION		$	
AUTOMOBILE EXPENSES		$	
CHARITABLE CONTRIBUTIONS		$	
DEPRECIATION		$	
EQUIPMENT RENTAL		$	
INSURANCE		$	
INTEREST EXPENSE		$	
LICENSES		$	
OFFICE SUPPLIES		$	
OFFICER COMPENSATION		$	
PAYROLL EXPENSES		$	
RENT		$	
TELEPHONE		$	
TRAVEL & ENTERTAINMENT		$	
UTILITIES		$	
WASTE DISPOSAL		$	
TOTAL OPERATING EXPENSE		$	
NET ORDINARY INCOME		$	
OTHER INCOME		$	
OTHER EXPENSES		$	
NET INCOME		$	

BUSINESS NAME

PROFIT AND LOSS STATEMENT – DATE: TO			
	$		$
	$		$
	$		$
	$		$
	$		$
TOTAL REVENUES	$		
COST OF GOODS SOLD	$		
GROSS PROFIT	$		
OPERATING EXPENSES			
ADVERTISING	$		
AMORTIZATION	$		
AUTOMOBILE EXPENSES	$		
CHARITABLE CONTRIBUTIONS	$		
DEPRECIATION	$		
EQUIPMENT RENTAL	$		
INSURANCE	$		
INTEREST EXPENSE	$		
LICENSES	$		
OFFICE SUPPLIES	$		
OFFICER COMPENSATION	$		
PAYROLL EXPENSES	$		
RENT	$		
TELEPHONE	$		
TRAVEL & ENTERTAINMENT	$		
UTILITIES	$		
WASTE DISPOSAL	$		
TOTAL OPERATING EXPENSE	$		
NET ORDINARY INCOME	$		
OTHER INCOME	$		
OTHER EXPENSES	$		
NET INCOME	$		

BUSINESS NAME

PROFIT AND LOSS STATEMENT - DATE: TO			
	$		$
	$		$
	$		$
	$		$
	$		$
TOTAL REVENUES	$		
COST OF GOODS SOLD	$		
GROSS PROFIT	$		
OPERATING EXPENSES			
ADVERTISING	$		
AMORTIZATION	$		
AUTOMOBILE EXPENSES	$		
CHARITABLE CONTRIBUTIONS	$		
DEPRECIATION	$		
EQUIPMENT RENTAL	$		
INSURANCE	$		
INTEREST EXPENSE	$		
LICENSES	$		
OFFICE SUPPLIES	$		
OFFICER COMPENSATION	$		
PAYROLL EXPENSES	$		
RENT	$		
TELEPHONE	$		
TRAVEL & ENTERTAINMENT	$		
UTILITIES	$		
WASTE DISPOSAL	$		
TOTAL OPERATING EXPENSE	$		
NET ORDINARY INCOME	$		
OTHER INCOME	$		
OTHER EXPENSES	$		
NET INCOME	$		

BUSINESS NAME

PROFIT AND LOSS STATEMENT - DATE: TO			
REVENUES			
	$		$
	$		$
	$		$
	$		$
	$		$
TOTAL REVENUES	$		
COST OF GOODS SOLD	$		
GROSS PROFIT	$		
OPERATING EXPENSES			
ADVERTISING	$		
AMORTIZATION	$		
AUTOMOBILE EXPENSES	$		
CHARITABLE CONTRIBUTIONS	$		
DEPRECIATION	$		
EQUIPMENT RENTAL	$		
INSURANCE	$		
INTEREST EXPENSE	$		
LICENSES	$		
OFFICE SUPPLIES	$		
OFFICER COMPENSATION	$		
PAYROLL EXPENSES	$		
RENT	$		
TELEPHONE	$		
TRAVEL & ENTERTAINMENT	$		
UTILITIES	$		
WASTE DISPOSAL	$		
TOTAL OPERATING EXPENSE	$		
NET ORDINARY INCOME	$		
OTHER INCOME	$		
OTHER EXPENSES	$		
NET INCOME	$		

BUSINESS NAME

PROFIT AND LOSS STATEMENT - DATE: TO			
	$		$
	$		$
	$		$
	$		$
	$		$
TOTAL REVENUES	$		
COST OF GOODS SOLD	$		
GROSS PROFIT	$		
OPERATING EXPENSES			
ADVERTISING	$		
AMORTIZATION	$		
AUTOMOBILE EXPENSES	$		
CHARITABLE CONTRIBUTIONS	$		
DEPRECIATION	$		
EQUIPMENT RENTAL	$		
INSURANCE	$		
INTEREST EXPENSE	$		
LICENSES	$		
OFFICE SUPPLIES	$		
OFFICER COMPENSATION	$		
PAYROLL EXPENSES	$		
RENT	$		
TELEPHONE	$		
TRAVEL & ENTERTAINMENT	$		
UTILITIES	$		
WASTE DISPOSAL	$		
TOTAL OPERATING EXPENSE	$		
NET ORDINARY INCOME	$		
OTHER INCOME	$		
OTHER EXPENSES	$		
NET INCOME	$		

BUSINESS NAME

PROFIT AND LOSS STATEMENT – DATE: TO			
REVENUES			
	$		$
	$		$
	$		$
	$		$
	$		$
TOTAL REVENUES	$		
COST OF GOODS SOLD	$		
GROSS PROFIT	$		
OPERATING EXPENSES			
ADVERTISING	$		
AMORTIZATION	$		
AUTOMOBILE EXPENSES	$		
CHARITABLE CONTRIBUTIONS	$		
DEPRECIATION	$		
EQUIPMENT RENTAL	$		
INSURANCE	$		
INTEREST EXPENSE	$		
LICENSES	$		
OFFICE SUPPLIES	$		
OFFICER COMPENSATION	$		
PAYROLL EXPENSES	$		
RENT	$		
TELEPHONE	$		
TRAVEL & ENTERTAINMENT	$		
UTILITIES	$		
WASTE DISPOSAL	$		
TOTAL OPERATING EXPENSE	$		
NET ORDINARY INCOME	$		
OTHER INCOME	$		
OTHER EXPENSES	$		
NET INCOME	$		

BUSINESS NAME

PROFIT AND LOSS STATEMENT – DATE: TO			
REVENUES			
	$		$
	$		$
	$		$
	$		$
	$		$
TOTAL REVENUES	$		
COST OF GOODS SOLD	$		
GROSS PROFIT	$		
OPERATING EXPENSES			
ADVERTISING	$		
AMORTIZATION	$		
AUTOMOBILE EXPENSES	$		
CHARITABLE CONTRIBUTIONS	$		
DEPRECIATION	$		
EQUIPMENT RENTAL	$		
INSURANCE	$		
INTEREST EXPENSE	$		
LICENSES	$		
OFFICE SUPPLIES	$		
OFFICER COMPENSATION	$		
PAYROLL EXPENSES	$		
RENT	$		
TELEPHONE	$		
TRAVEL & ENTERTAINMENT	$		
UTILITIES	$		
WASTE DISPOSAL	$		
TOTAL OPERATING EXPENSE	$		
NET ORDINARY INCOME	$		
OTHER INCOME	$		
OTHER EXPENSES	$		
NET INCOME	$		

BUSINESS NAME

PROFIT AND LOSS STATEMENT – DATE: TO			
	$		$
	$		$
	$		$
	$		$
	$		$
TOTAL REVENUES		$	
COST OF GOODS SOLD		$	
GROSS PROFIT		$	
OPERATING EXPENSES			
ADVERTISING		$	
AMORTIZATION		$	
AUTOMOBILE EXPENSES		$	
CHARITABLE CONTRIBUTIONS		$	
DEPRECIATION		$	
EQUIPMENT RENTAL		$	
INSURANCE		$	
INTEREST EXPENSE		$	
LICENSES		$	
OFFICE SUPPLIES		$	
OFFICER COMPENSATION		$	
PAYROLL EXPENSES		$	
RENT		$	
TELEPHONE		$	
TRAVEL & ENTERTAINMENT		$	
UTILITIES		$	
WASTE DISPOSAL		$	
TOTAL OPERATING EXPENSE		$	
NET ORDINARY INCOME		$	
OTHER INCOME		$	
OTHER EXPENSES		$	
NET INCOME		$	

BUSINESS NAME

PROFIT AND LOSS STATEMENT — DATE:		TO	
\multicolumn{4}{c}{REVENUES}			
	$		$
	$		$
	$		$
	$		$
	$		$
TOTAL REVENUES	$		
COST OF GOODS SOLD	$		
GROSS PROFIT	$		
\multicolumn{4}{c}{OPERATING EXPENSES}			
ADVERTISING	$		
AMORTIZATION	$		
AUTOMOBILE EXPENSES	$		
CHARITABLE CONTRIBUTIONS	$		
DEPRECIATION	$		
EQUIPMENT RENTAL	$		
INSURANCE	$		
INTEREST EXPENSE	$		
LICENSES	$		
OFFICE SUPPLIES	$		
OFFICER COMPENSATION	$		
PAYROLL EXPENSES	$		
RENT	$		
TELEPHONE	$		
TRAVEL & ENTERTAINMENT	$		
UTILITIES	$		
WASTE DISPOSAL	$		
TOTAL OPERATING EXPENSE	$		
NET ORDINARY INCOME	$		
OTHER INCOME	$		
OTHER EXPENSES	$		
NET INCOME	$		

BUSINESS NAME

PROFIT AND LOSS STATEMENT – DATE: TO			
REVENUES			
	$		$
	$		$
	$		$
	$		$
	$		$
TOTAL REVENUES	$		
COST OF GOODS SOLD	$		
GROSS PROFIT	$		
OPERATING EXPENSES			
ADVERTISING	$		
AMORTIZATION	$		
AUTOMOBILE EXPENSES	$		
CHARITABLE CONTRIBUTIONS	$		
DEPRECIATION	$		
EQUIPMENT RENTAL	$		
INSURANCE	$		
INTEREST EXPENSE	$		
LICENSES	$		
OFFICE SUPPLIES	$		
OFFICER COMPENSATION	$		
PAYROLL EXPENSES	$		
RENT	$		
TELEPHONE	$		
TRAVEL & ENTERTAINMENT	$		
UTILITIES	$		
WASTE DISPOSAL	$		
TOTAL OPERATING EXPENSE	$		
NET ORDINARY INCOME	$		
OTHER INCOME	$		
OTHER EXPENSES	$		
NET INCOME	$		

BUSINESS NAME

PROFIT AND LOSS STATEMENT − DATE: TO			
REVENUES			
	$		$
	$		$
	$		$
	$		$
	$		$
TOTAL REVENUES		$	
COST OF GOODS SOLD		$	
GROSS PROFIT		$	
OPERATING EXPENSES			
ADVERTISING		$	
AMORTIZATION		$	
AUTOMOBILE EXPENSES		$	
CHARITABLE CONTRIBUTIONS		$	
DEPRECIATION		$	
EQUIPMENT RENTAL		$	
INSURANCE		$	
INTEREST EXPENSE		$	
LICENSES		$	
OFFICE SUPPLIES		$	
OFFICER COMPENSATION		$	
PAYROLL EXPENSES		$	
RENT		$	
TELEPHONE		$	
TRAVEL & ENTERTAINMENT		$	
UTILITIES		$	
WASTE DISPOSAL		$	
TOTAL OPERATING EXPENSE		$	
NET ORDINARY INCOME		$	
OTHER INCOME		$	
OTHER EXPENSES		$	
NET INCOME		$	

BUSINESS NAME

PROFIT AND LOSS STATEMENT – DATE: TO				
	$			$
	$			$
	$			$
	$			$
	$			$
TOTAL REVENUES		$		
COST OF GOODS SOLD		$		
GROSS PROFIT		$		
OPERATING EXPENSES				
ADVERTISING		$		
AMORTIZATION		$		
AUTOMOBILE EXPENSES		$		
CHARITABLE CONTRIBUTIONS		$		
DEPRECIATION		$		
EQUIPMENT RENTAL		$		
INSURANCE		$		
INTEREST EXPENSE		$		
LICENSES		$		
OFFICE SUPPLIES		$		
OFFICER COMPENSATION		$		
PAYROLL EXPENSES		$		
RENT		$		
TELEPHONE		$		
TRAVEL & ENTERTAINMENT		$		
UTILITIES		$		
WASTE DISPOSAL		$		
TOTAL OPERATING EXPENSE		$		
NET ORDINARY INCOME		$		
OTHER INCOME		$		
OTHER EXPENSES		$		
NET INCOME		$		

BUSINESS NAME

PROFIT AND LOSS STATEMENT – DATE: TO				
	$			$
	$			$
	$			$
	$			$
	$			$
TOTAL REVENUES		$		
COST OF GOODS SOLD		$		
GROSS PROFIT		$		
OPERATING EXPENSES				
ADVERTISING		$		
AMORTIZATION		$		
AUTOMOBILE EXPENSES		$		
CHARITABLE CONTRIBUTIONS		$		
DEPRECIATION		$		
EQUIPMENT RENTAL		$		
INSURANCE		$		
INTEREST EXPENSE		$		
LICENSES		$		
OFFICE SUPPLIES		$		
OFFICER COMPENSATION		$		
PAYROLL EXPENSES		$		
RENT		$		
TELEPHONE		$		
TRAVEL & ENTERTAINMENT		$		
UTILITIES		$		
WASTE DISPOSAL		$		
TOTAL OPERATING EXPENSE		$		
NET ORDINARY INCOME		$		
OTHER INCOME		$		
OTHER EXPENSES		$		
NET INCOME		$		

BUSINESS NAME

PROFIT AND LOSS STATEMENT — DATE: TO				
	$			$
	$			$
	$			$
	$			$
	$			$
TOTAL REVENUES		$		
COST OF GOODS SOLD		$		
GROSS PROFIT		$		
OPERATING EXPENSES				
ADVERTISING		$		
AMORTIZATION		$		
AUTOMOBILE EXPENSES		$		
CHARITABLE CONTRIBUTIONS		$		
DEPRECIATION		$		
EQUIPMENT RENTAL		$		
INSURANCE		$		
INTEREST EXPENSE		$		
LICENSES		$		
OFFICE SUPPLIES		$		
OFFICER COMPENSATION		$		
PAYROLL EXPENSES		$		
RENT		$		
TELEPHONE		$		
TRAVEL & ENTERTAINMENT		$		
UTILITIES		$		
WASTE DISPOSAL		$		
TOTAL OPERATING EXPENSE		$		
NET ORDINARY INCOME		$		
OTHER INCOME		$		
OTHER EXPENSES		$		
NET INCOME		$		

BUSINESS NAME

PROFIT AND LOSS STATEMENT – DATE: TO			
REVENUES			
	$		$
	$		$
	$		$
	$		$
	$		$
TOTAL REVENUES	$		
COST OF GOODS SOLD	$		
GROSS PROFIT	$		
OPERATING EXPENSES			
ADVERTISING	$		
AMORTIZATION	$		
AUTOMOBILE EXPENSES	$		
CHARITABLE CONTRIBUTIONS	$		
DEPRECIATION	$		
EQUIPMENT RENTAL	$		
INSURANCE	$		
INTEREST EXPENSE	$		
LICENSES	$		
OFFICE SUPPLIES	$		
OFFICER COMPENSATION	$		
PAYROLL EXPENSES	$		
RENT	$		
TELEPHONE	$		
TRAVEL & ENTERTAINMENT	$		
UTILITIES	$		
WASTE DISPOSAL	$		
TOTAL OPERATING EXPENSE	$		
NET ORDINARY INCOME	$		
OTHER INCOME	$		
OTHER EXPENSES	$		
NET INCOME	$		

BUSINESS NAME

PROFIT AND LOSS STATEMENT – DATE: TO			
REVENUES			
	$		$
	$		$
	$		$
	$		$
	$		$
TOTAL REVENUES	$		
COST OF GOODS SOLD	$		
GROSS PROFIT	$		
OPERATING EXPENSES			
ADVERTISING	$		
AMORTIZATION	$		
AUTOMOBILE EXPENSES	$		
CHARITABLE CONTRIBUTIONS	$		
DEPRECIATION	$		
EQUIPMENT RENTAL	$		
INSURANCE	$		
INTEREST EXPENSE	$		
LICENSES	$		
OFFICE SUPPLIES	$		
OFFICER COMPENSATION	$		
PAYROLL EXPENSES	$		
RENT	$		
TELEPHONE	$		
TRAVEL & ENTERTAINMENT	$		
UTILITIES	$		
WASTE DISPOSAL	$		
TOTAL OPERATING EXPENSE	$		
NET ORDINARY INCOME	$		
OTHER INCOME	$		
OTHER EXPENSES	$		
NET INCOME	$		

BUSINESS NAME

PROFIT AND LOSS STATEMENT – DATE: TO				
	$		$	
	$		$	
	$		$	
	$		$	
	$		$	
TOTAL REVENUES		$		
COST OF GOODS SOLD		$		
GROSS PROFIT		$		
OPERATING EXPENSES				
ADVERTISING		$		
AMORTIZATION		$		
AUTOMOBILE EXPENSES		$		
CHARITABLE CONTRIBUTIONS		$		
DEPRECIATION		$		
EQUIPMENT RENTAL		$		
INSURANCE		$		
INTEREST EXPENSE		$		
LICENSES		$		
OFFICE SUPPLIES		$		
OFFICER COMPENSATION		$		
PAYROLL EXPENSES		$		
RENT		$		
TELEPHONE		$		
TRAVEL & ENTERTAINMENT		$		
UTILITIES		$		
WASTE DISPOSAL		$		
TOTAL OPERATING EXPENSE		$		
NET ORDINARY INCOME		$		
OTHER INCOME		$		
OTHER EXPENSES		$		
NET INCOME		$		

BUSINESS NAME

PROFIT AND LOSS STATEMENT – DATE: TO			
REVENUES			
	$		$
	$		$
	$		$
	$		$
	$		$
TOTAL REVENUES	$		
COST OF GOODS SOLD	$		
GROSS PROFIT	$		
OPERATING EXPENSES			
ADVERTISING	$		
AMORTIZATION	$		
AUTOMOBILE EXPENSES	$		
CHARITABLE CONTRIBUTIONS	$		
DEPRECIATION	$		
EQUIPMENT RENTAL	$		
INSURANCE	$		
INTEREST EXPENSE	$		
LICENSES	$		
OFFICE SUPPLIES	$		
OFFICER COMPENSATION	$		
PAYROLL EXPENSES	$		
RENT	$		
TELEPHONE	$		
TRAVEL & ENTERTAINMENT	$		
UTILITIES	$		
WASTE DISPOSAL	$		
TOTAL OPERATING EXPENSE	$		
NET ORDINARY INCOME	$		
OTHER INCOME	$		
OTHER EXPENSES	$		
NET INCOME	$		

BUSINESS NAME

PROFIT AND LOSS STATEMENT – DATE: TO			
	$		$
	$		$
	$		$
	$		$
	$		$
TOTAL REVENUES	$		
COST OF GOODS SOLD	$		
GROSS PROFIT	$		
OPERATING EXPENSES			
ADVERTISING	$		
AMORTIZATION	$		
AUTOMOBILE EXPENSES	$		
CHARITABLE CONTRIBUTIONS	$		
DEPRECIATION	$		
EQUIPMENT RENTAL	$		
INSURANCE	$		
INTEREST EXPENSE	$		
LICENSES	$		
OFFICE SUPPLIES	$		
OFFICER COMPENSATION	$		
PAYROLL EXPENSES	$		
RENT	$		
TELEPHONE	$		
TRAVEL & ENTERTAINMENT	$		
UTILITIES	$		
WASTE DISPOSAL	$		
TOTAL OPERATING EXPENSE	$		
NET ORDINARY INCOME	$		
OTHER INCOME	$		
OTHER EXPENSES	$		
NET INCOME	$		

BUSINESS NAME

PROFIT AND LOSS STATEMENT – DATE: TO			
	REVENUES			
	$		$
	$		$
	$		$
	$		$
	$		$
TOTAL REVENUES	$		
COST OF GOODS SOLD	$		
GROSS PROFIT	$		
	OPERATING EXPENSES			
ADVERTISING	$		
AMORTIZATION	$		
AUTOMOBILE EXPENSES	$		
CHARITABLE CONTRIBUTIONS	$		
DEPRECIATION	$		
EQUIPMENT RENTAL	$		
INSURANCE	$		
INTEREST EXPENSE	$		
LICENSES	$		
OFFICE SUPPLIES	$		
OFFICER COMPENSATION	$		
PAYROLL EXPENSES	$		
RENT	$		
TELEPHONE	$		
TRAVEL & ENTERTAINMENT	$		
UTILITIES	$		
WASTE DISPOSAL	$		
TOTAL OPERATING EXPENSE	$		
NET ORDINARY INCOME	$		
OTHER INCOME	$		
OTHER EXPENSES	$		
NET INCOME	$		

BUSINESS NAME

PROFIT AND LOSS STATEMENT – DATE: TO			
	REVENUES			
	$		$
	$		$
	$		$
	$		$
	$		$
TOTAL REVENUES	$		
COST OF GOODS SOLD	$		
GROSS PROFIT	$		
	OPERATING EXPENSES			
ADVERTISING	$		
AMORTIZATION	$		
AUTOMOBILE EXPENSES	$		
CHARITABLE CONTRIBUTIONS	$		
DEPRECIATION	$		
EQUIPMENT RENTAL	$		
INSURANCE	$		
INTEREST EXPENSE	$		
LICENSES	$		
OFFICE SUPPLIES	$		
OFFICER COMPENSATION	$		
PAYROLL EXPENSES	$		
RENT	$		
TELEPHONE	$		
TRAVEL & ENTERTAINMENT	$		
UTILITIES	$		
WASTE DISPOSAL	$		
TOTAL OPERATING EXPENSE	$		
NET ORDINARY INCOME	$		
OTHER INCOME	$		
OTHER EXPENSES	$		
NET INCOME	$		

BUSINESS NAME

PROFIT AND LOSS STATEMENT – DATE: TO			
REVENUES			
	$		$
	$		$
	$		$
	$		$
	$		$
TOTAL REVENUES	$		
COST OF GOODS SOLD	$		
GROSS PROFIT	$		
OPERATING EXPENSES			
ADVERTISING	$		
AMORTIZATION	$		
AUTOMOBILE EXPENSES	$		
CHARITABLE CONTRIBUTIONS	$		
DEPRECIATION	$		
EQUIPMENT RENTAL	$		
INSURANCE	$		
INTEREST EXPENSE	$		
LICENSES	$		
OFFICE SUPPLIES	$		
OFFICER COMPENSATION	$		
PAYROLL EXPENSES	$		
RENT	$		
TELEPHONE	$		
TRAVEL & ENTERTAINMENT	$		
UTILITIES	$		
WASTE DISPOSAL	$		
TOTAL OPERATING EXPENSE	$		
NET ORDINARY INCOME	$		
OTHER INCOME	$		
OTHER EXPENSES	$		
NET INCOME	$		

BUSINESS NAME

PROFIT AND LOSS STATEMENT - DATE: TO				
REVENUES				
	$		$	
	$		$	
	$		$	
	$		$	
	$		$	
TOTAL REVENUES	$			
COST OF GOODS SOLD	$			
GROSS PROFIT	$			
OPERATING EXPENSES				
ADVERTISING	$			
AMORTIZATION	$			
AUTOMOBILE EXPENSES	$			
CHARITABLE CONTRIBUTIONS	$			
DEPRECIATION	$			
EQUIPMENT RENTAL	$			
INSURANCE	$			
INTEREST EXPENSE	$			
LICENSES	$			
OFFICE SUPPLIES	$			
OFFICER COMPENSATION	$			
PAYROLL EXPENSES	$			
RENT	$			
TELEPHONE	$			
TRAVEL & ENTERTAINMENT	$			
UTILITIES	$			
WASTE DISPOSAL	$			
TOTAL OPERATING EXPENSE	$			
NET ORDINARY INCOME	$			
OTHER INCOME	$			
OTHER EXPENSES	$			
NET INCOME	$			

BUSINESS NAME

PROFIT AND LOSS STATEMENT – DATE: TO			
	$		$
	$		$
	$		$
	$		$
	$		$
TOTAL REVENUES	$		
COST OF GOODS SOLD	$		
GROSS PROFIT	$		
OPERATING EXPENSES			
ADVERTISING	$		
AMORTIZATION	$		
AUTOMOBILE EXPENSES	$		
CHARITABLE CONTRIBUTIONS	$		
DEPRECIATION	$		
EQUIPMENT RENTAL	$		
INSURANCE	$		
INTEREST EXPENSE	$		
LICENSES	$		
OFFICE SUPPLIES	$		
OFFICER COMPENSATION	$		
PAYROLL EXPENSES	$		
RENT	$		
TELEPHONE	$		
TRAVEL & ENTERTAINMENT	$		
UTILITIES	$		
WASTE DISPOSAL	$		
TOTAL OPERATING EXPENSE	$		
NET ORDINARY INCOME	$		
OTHER INCOME	$		
OTHER EXPENSES	$		
NET INCOME	$		

BUSINESS NAME

PROFIT AND LOSS STATEMENT - DATE: TO			
REVENUES			
	$		$
	$		$
	$		$
	$		$
	$		$
TOTAL REVENUES	$		
COST OF GOODS SOLD	$		
GROSS PROFIT	$		
OPERATING EXPENSES			
ADVERTISING	$		
AMORTIZATION	$		
AUTOMOBILE EXPENSES	$		
CHARITABLE CONTRIBUTIONS	$		
DEPRECIATION	$		
EQUIPMENT RENTAL	$		
INSURANCE	$		
INTEREST EXPENSE	$		
LICENSES	$		
OFFICE SUPPLIES	$		
OFFICER COMPENSATION	$		
PAYROLL EXPENSES	$		
RENT	$		
TELEPHONE	$		
TRAVEL & ENTERTAINMENT	$		
UTILITIES	$		
WASTE DISPOSAL	$		
TOTAL OPERATING EXPENSE	$		
NET ORDINARY INCOME	$		
OTHER INCOME	$		
OTHER EXPENSES	$		
NET INCOME	$		

BUSINESS NAME

PROFIT AND LOSS STATEMENT – DATE: TO				
	$			$
	$			$
	$			$
	$			$
	$			$
TOTAL REVENUES		$		
COST OF GOODS SOLD		$		
GROSS PROFIT		$		
OPERATING EXPENSES				
ADVERTISING		$		
AMORTIZATION		$		
AUTOMOBILE EXPENSES		$		
CHARITABLE CONTRIBUTIONS		$		
DEPRECIATION		$		
EQUIPMENT RENTAL		$		
INSURANCE		$		
INTEREST EXPENSE		$		
LICENSES		$		
OFFICE SUPPLIES		$		
OFFICER COMPENSATION		$		
PAYROLL EXPENSES		$		
RENT		$		
TELEPHONE		$		
TRAVEL & ENTERTAINMENT		$		
UTILITIES		$		
WASTE DISPOSAL		$		
TOTAL OPERATING EXPENSE		$		
NET ORDINARY INCOME		$		
OTHER INCOME		$		
OTHER EXPENSES		$		
NET INCOME		$		

BUSINESS NAME

PROFIT AND LOSS STATEMENT − DATE: TO			
REVENUES			
	$		$
	$		$
	$		$
	$		$
	$		$
TOTAL REVENUES	$		
COST OF GOODS SOLD	$		
GROSS PROFIT	$		
OPERATING EXPENSES			
ADVERTISING	$		
AMORTIZATION	$		
AUTOMOBILE EXPENSES	$		
CHARITABLE CONTRIBUTIONS	$		
DEPRECIATION	$		
EQUIPMENT RENTAL	$		
INSURANCE	$		
INTEREST EXPENSE	$		
LICENSES	$		
OFFICE SUPPLIES	$		
OFFICER COMPENSATION	$		
PAYROLL EXPENSES	$		
RENT	$		
TELEPHONE	$		
TRAVEL & ENTERTAINMENT	$		
UTILITIES	$		
WASTE DISPOSAL	$		
TOTAL OPERATING EXPENSE	$		
NET ORDINARY INCOME	$		
OTHER INCOME	$		
OTHER EXPENSES	$		
NET INCOME	$		

BUSINESS NAME

PROFIT AND LOSS STATEMENT – DATE: TO			
	REVENUES		
	$		$
	$		$
	$		$
	$		$
	$		$
TOTAL REVENUES	$		
COST OF GOODS SOLD	$		
GROSS PROFIT	$		
OPERATING EXPENSES			
ADVERTISING	$		
AMORTIZATION	$		
AUTOMOBILE EXPENSES	$		
CHARITABLE CONTRIBUTIONS	$		
DEPRECIATION	$		
EQUIPMENT RENTAL	$		
INSURANCE	$		
INTEREST EXPENSE	$		
LICENSES	$		
OFFICE SUPPLIES	$		
OFFICER COMPENSATION	$		
PAYROLL EXPENSES	$		
RENT	$		
TELEPHONE	$		
TRAVEL & ENTERTAINMENT	$		
UTILITIES	$		
WASTE DISPOSAL	$		
TOTAL OPERATING EXPENSE	$		
NET ORDINARY INCOME	$		
OTHER INCOME	$		
OTHER EXPENSES	$		
NET INCOME	$		

BUSINESS NAME

PROFIT AND LOSS STATEMENT - DATE: TO				
	$		$	
	$		$	
	$		$	
	$		$	
	$		$	
TOTAL REVENUES		$		
COST OF GOODS SOLD		$		
GROSS PROFIT		$		
OPERATING EXPENSES				
ADVERTISING		$		
AMORTIZATION		$		
AUTOMOBILE EXPENSES		$		
CHARITABLE CONTRIBUTIONS		$		
DEPRECIATION		$		
EQUIPMENT RENTAL		$		
INSURANCE		$		
INTEREST EXPENSE		$		
LICENSES		$		
OFFICE SUPPLIES		$		
OFFICER COMPENSATION		$		
PAYROLL EXPENSES		$		
RENT		$		
TELEPHONE		$		
TRAVEL & ENTERTAINMENT		$		
UTILITIES		$		
WASTE DISPOSAL		$		
TOTAL OPERATING EXPENSE		$		
NET ORDINARY INCOME		$		
OTHER INCOME		$		
OTHER EXPENSES		$		
NET INCOME		$		

BUSINESS NAME

PROFIT AND LOSS STATEMENT - DATE: TO			
REVENUES			
	$		$
	$		$
	$		$
	$		$
	$		$
TOTAL REVENUES		$	
COST OF GOODS SOLD		$	
GROSS PROFIT		$	
OPERATING EXPENSES			
ADVERTISING		$	
AMORTIZATION		$	
AUTOMOBILE EXPENSES		$	
CHARITABLE CONTRIBUTIONS		$	
DEPRECIATION		$	
EQUIPMENT RENTAL		$	
INSURANCE		$	
INTEREST EXPENSE		$	
LICENSES		$	
OFFICE SUPPLIES		$	
OFFICER COMPENSATION		$	
PAYROLL EXPENSES		$	
RENT		$	
TELEPHONE		$	
TRAVEL & ENTERTAINMENT		$	
UTILITIES		$	
WASTE DISPOSAL		$	
TOTAL OPERATING EXPENSE		$	
NET ORDINARY INCOME		$	
OTHER INCOME		$	
OTHER EXPENSES		$	
NET INCOME		$	

BUSINESS NAME

PROFIT AND LOSS STATEMENT – DATE: TO			
	$		$
	$		$
	$		$
	$		$
	$		$
TOTAL REVENUES	$		
COST OF GOODS SOLD	$		
GROSS PROFIT	$		
OPERATING EXPENSES			
ADVERTISING	$		
AMORTIZATION	$		
AUTOMOBILE EXPENSES	$		
CHARITABLE CONTRIBUTIONS	$		
DEPRECIATION	$		
EQUIPMENT RENTAL	$		
INSURANCE	$		
INTEREST EXPENSE	$		
LICENSES	$		
OFFICE SUPPLIES	$		
OFFICER COMPENSATION	$		
PAYROLL EXPENSES	$		
RENT	$		
TELEPHONE	$		
TRAVEL & ENTERTAINMENT	$		
UTILITIES	$		
WASTE DISPOSAL	$		
TOTAL OPERATING EXPENSE	$		
NET ORDINARY INCOME	$		
OTHER INCOME	$		
OTHER EXPENSES	$		
NET INCOME	$		

BUSINESS NAME

PROFIT AND LOSS STATEMENT - DATE: TO			
REVENUES			
	$		$
	$		$
	$		$
	$		$
	$		$

TOTAL REVENUES	$
COST OF GOODS SOLD	$
GROSS PROFIT	$
OPERATING EXPENSES	
ADVERTISING	$
AMORTIZATION	$
AUTOMOBILE EXPENSES	$
CHARITABLE CONTRIBUTIONS	$
DEPRECIATION	$
EQUIPMENT RENTAL	$
INSURANCE	$
INTEREST EXPENSE	$
LICENSES	$
OFFICE SUPPLIES	$
OFFICER COMPENSATION	$
PAYROLL EXPENSES	$
RENT	$
TELEPHONE	$
TRAVEL & ENTERTAINMENT	$
UTILITIES	$
WASTE DISPOSAL	$
TOTAL OPERATING EXPENSE	$
NET ORDINARY INCOME	$
OTHER INCOME	$
OTHER EXPENSES	$
NET INCOME	$

BUSINESS NAME

PROFIT AND LOSS STATEMENT - DATE: TO			
REVENUES			
	$		$
	$		$
	$		$
	$		$
	$		$
TOTAL REVENUES	$		
COST OF GOODS SOLD	$		
GROSS PROFIT	$		
OPERATING EXPENSES			
ADVERTISING	$		
AMORTIZATION	$		
AUTOMOBILE EXPENSES	$		
CHARITABLE CONTRIBUTIONS	$		
DEPRECIATION	$		
EQUIPMENT RENTAL	$		
INSURANCE	$		
INTEREST EXPENSE	$		
LICENSES	$		
OFFICE SUPPLIES	$		
OFFICER COMPENSATION	$		
PAYROLL EXPENSES	$		
RENT	$		
TELEPHONE	$		
TRAVEL & ENTERTAINMENT	$		
UTILITIES	$		
WASTE DISPOSAL	$		
TOTAL OPERATING EXPENSE	$		
NET ORDINARY INCOME	$		
OTHER INCOME	$		
OTHER EXPENSES	$		
NET INCOME	$		

BUSINESS NAME

PROFIT AND LOSS STATEMENT – DATE: TO			
REVENUES			
	$		$
	$		$
	$		$
	$		$
	$		$
TOTAL REVENUES	$		
COST OF GOODS SOLD	$		
GROSS PROFIT	$		
OPERATING EXPENSES			
ADVERTISING	$		
AMORTIZATION	$		
AUTOMOBILE EXPENSES	$		
CHARITABLE CONTRIBUTIONS	$		
DEPRECIATION	$		
EQUIPMENT RENTAL	$		
INSURANCE	$		
INTEREST EXPENSE	$		
LICENSES	$		
OFFICE SUPPLIES	$		
OFFICER COMPENSATION	$		
PAYROLL EXPENSES	$		
RENT	$		
TELEPHONE	$		
TRAVEL & ENTERTAINMENT	$		
UTILITIES	$		
WASTE DISPOSAL	$		
TOTAL OPERATING EXPENSE	$		
NET ORDINARY INCOME	$		
OTHER INCOME	$		
OTHER EXPENSES	$		
NET INCOME	$		

BUSINESS NAME

PROFIT AND LOSS STATEMENT − DATE: TO				
REVENUES				
	$			$
	$			$
	$			$
	$			$
	$			$
TOTAL REVENUES	$		
COST OF GOODS SOLD	$		
GROSS PROFIT	$		
**OPERATING EXPENSES**				
ADVERTISING	$		
AMORTIZATION	$		
AUTOMOBILE EXPENSES	$		
CHARITABLE CONTRIBUTIONS	$		
DEPRECIATION	$		
EQUIPMENT RENTAL	$		
INSURANCE	$		
INTEREST EXPENSE	$		
LICENSES	$		
OFFICE SUPPLIES	$		
OFFICER COMPENSATION	$		
PAYROLL EXPENSES	$		
RENT	$		
TELEPHONE	$		
TRAVEL & ENTERTAINMENT	$		
UTILITIES	$		
WASTE DISPOSAL	$		
TOTAL OPERATING EXPENSE	$		
NET ORDINARY INCOME	$		
OTHER INCOME	$		
OTHER EXPENSES	$		
NET INCOME	$		

BUSINESS NAME

PROFIT AND LOSS STATEMENT – DATE: TO			
	$		$
	$		$
	$		$
	$		$
	$		$
TOTAL REVENUES	$		
COST OF GOODS SOLD	$		
GROSS PROFIT	$		
OPERATING EXPENSES			
ADVERTISING	$		
AMORTIZATION	$		
AUTOMOBILE EXPENSES	$		
CHARITABLE CONTRIBUTIONS	$		
DEPRECIATION	$		
EQUIPMENT RENTAL	$		
INSURANCE	$		
INTEREST EXPENSE	$		
LICENSES	$		
OFFICE SUPPLIES	$		
OFFICER COMPENSATION	$		
PAYROLL EXPENSES	$		
RENT	$		
TELEPHONE	$		
TRAVEL & ENTERTAINMENT	$		
UTILITIES	$		
WASTE DISPOSAL	$		
TOTAL OPERATING EXPENSE	$		
NET ORDINARY INCOME	$		
OTHER INCOME	$		
OTHER EXPENSES	$		
NET INCOME	$		

BUSINESS NAME

PROFIT AND LOSS STATEMENT – DATE: TO			
	$		$
	$		$
	$		$
	$		$
	$		$
TOTAL REVENUES		$	
COST OF GOODS SOLD		$	
GROSS PROFIT		$	
OPERATING EXPENSES			
ADVERTISING		$	
AMORTIZATION		$	
AUTOMOBILE EXPENSES		$	
CHARITABLE CONTRIBUTIONS		$	
DEPRECIATION		$	
EQUIPMENT RENTAL		$	
INSURANCE		$	
INTEREST EXPENSE		$	
LICENSES		$	
OFFICE SUPPLIES		$	
OFFICER COMPENSATION		$	
PAYROLL EXPENSES		$	
RENT		$	
TELEPHONE		$	
TRAVEL & ENTERTAINMENT		$	
UTILITIES		$	
WASTE DISPOSAL		$	
TOTAL OPERATING EXPENSE		$	
NET ORDINARY INCOME		$	
OTHER INCOME		$	
OTHER EXPENSES		$	
NET INCOME		$	

BUSINESS NAME

PROFIT AND LOSS STATEMENT – DATE: TO			
\multicolumn{4}{c}{**REVENUES**}			
	$		$
	$		$
	$		$
	$		$
	$		$
TOTAL REVENUES	$		
COST OF GOODS SOLD	$		
GROSS PROFIT	$		
\multicolumn{4}{c}{**OPERATING EXPENSES**}			
ADVERTISING	$		
AMORTIZATION	$		
AUTOMOBILE EXPENSES	$		
CHARITABLE CONTRIBUTIONS	$		
DEPRECIATION	$		
EQUIPMENT RENTAL	$		
INSURANCE	$		
INTEREST EXPENSE	$		
LICENSES	$		
OFFICE SUPPLIES	$		
OFFICER COMPENSATION	$		
PAYROLL EXPENSES	$		
RENT	$		
TELEPHONE	$		
TRAVEL & ENTERTAINMENT	$		
UTILITIES	$		
WASTE DISPOSAL	$		
TOTAL OPERATING EXPENSE	$		
NET ORDINARY INCOME	$		
OTHER INCOME	$		
OTHER EXPENSES	$		
NET INCOME	$		

BUSINESS NAME

PROFIT AND LOSS STATEMENT – DATE: TO			
REVENUES			
	$		$
	$		$
	$		$
	$		$
	$		$
TOTAL REVENUES	$		
COST OF GOODS SOLD	$		
GROSS PROFIT	$		
OPERATING EXPENSES			
ADVERTISING	$		
AMORTIZATION	$		
AUTOMOBILE EXPENSES	$		
CHARITABLE CONTRIBUTIONS	$		
DEPRECIATION	$		
EQUIPMENT RENTAL	$		
INSURANCE	$		
INTEREST EXPENSE	$		
LICENSES	$		
OFFICE SUPPLIES	$		
OFFICER COMPENSATION	$		
PAYROLL EXPENSES	$		
RENT	$		
TELEPHONE	$		
TRAVEL & ENTERTAINMENT	$		
UTILITIES	$		
WASTE DISPOSAL	$		
TOTAL OPERATING EXPENSE	$		
NET ORDINARY INCOME	$		
OTHER INCOME	$		
OTHER EXPENSES	$		
NET INCOME	$		

BUSINESS NAME

PROFIT AND LOSS STATEMENT – DATE: TO			
REVENUES			
	$		$
	$		$
	$		$
	$		$
	$		$
TOTAL REVENUES		$	
COST OF GOODS SOLD		$	
GROSS PROFIT		$	
OPERATING EXPENSES			
ADVERTISING		$	
AMORTIZATION		$	
AUTOMOBILE EXPENSES		$	
CHARITABLE CONTRIBUTIONS		$	
DEPRECIATION		$	
EQUIPMENT RENTAL		$	
INSURANCE		$	
INTEREST EXPENSE		$	
LICENSES		$	
OFFICE SUPPLIES		$	
OFFICER COMPENSATION		$	
PAYROLL EXPENSES		$	
RENT		$	
TELEPHONE		$	
TRAVEL & ENTERTAINMENT		$	
UTILITIES		$	
WASTE DISPOSAL		$	
TOTAL OPERATING EXPENSE		$	
NET ORDINARY INCOME		$	
OTHER INCOME		$	
OTHER EXPENSES		$	
NET INCOME		$	

BUSINESS NAME

PROFIT AND LOSS STATEMENT - DATE: TO				
	$		$	
	$		$	
	$		$	
	$		$	
	$		$	
TOTAL REVENUES		$		
COST OF GOODS SOLD		$		
GROSS PROFIT		$		
OPERATING EXPENSES				
ADVERTISING		$		
AMORTIZATION		$		
AUTOMOBILE EXPENSES		$		
CHARITABLE CONTRIBUTIONS		$		
DEPRECIATION		$		
EQUIPMENT RENTAL		$		
INSURANCE		$		
INTEREST EXPENSE		$		
LICENSES		$		
OFFICE SUPPLIES		$		
OFFICER COMPENSATION		$		
PAYROLL EXPENSES		$		
RENT		$		
TELEPHONE		$		
TRAVEL & ENTERTAINMENT		$		
UTILITIES		$		
WASTE DISPOSAL		$		
TOTAL OPERATING EXPENSE		$		
NET ORDINARY INCOME		$		
OTHER INCOME		$		
OTHER EXPENSES		$		
NET INCOME		$		

BUSINESS NAME

PROFIT AND LOSS STATEMENT – DATE: TO			
	$		$
	$		$
	$		$
	$		$
	$		$
TOTAL REVENUES	$		
COST OF GOODS SOLD	$		
GROSS PROFIT	$		
OPERATING EXPENSES			
ADVERTISING	$		
AMORTIZATION	$		
AUTOMOBILE EXPENSES	$		
CHARITABLE CONTRIBUTIONS	$		
DEPRECIATION	$		
EQUIPMENT RENTAL	$		
INSURANCE	$		
INTEREST EXPENSE	$		
LICENSES	$		
OFFICE SUPPLIES	$		
OFFICER COMPENSATION	$		
PAYROLL EXPENSES	$		
RENT	$		
TELEPHONE	$		
TRAVEL & ENTERTAINMENT	$		
UTILITIES	$		
WASTE DISPOSAL	$		
TOTAL OPERATING EXPENSE	$		
NET ORDINARY INCOME	$		
OTHER INCOME	$		
OTHER EXPENSES	$		
NET INCOME	$		

BUSINESS NAME

PROFIT AND LOSS STATEMENT – DATE: TO			
REVENUES			
	$		$
	$		$
	$		$
	$		$
	$		$
TOTAL REVENUES	$		
COST OF GOODS SOLD	$		
GROSS PROFIT	$		
OPERATING EXPENSES			
ADVERTISING	$		
AMORTIZATION	$		
AUTOMOBILE EXPENSES	$		
CHARITABLE CONTRIBUTIONS	$		
DEPRECIATION	$		
EQUIPMENT RENTAL	$		
INSURANCE	$		
INTEREST EXPENSE	$		
LICENSES	$		
OFFICE SUPPLIES	$		
OFFICER COMPENSATION	$		
PAYROLL EXPENSES	$		
RENT	$		
TELEPHONE	$		
TRAVEL & ENTERTAINMENT	$		
UTILITIES	$		
WASTE DISPOSAL	$		
TOTAL OPERATING EXPENSE	$		
NET ORDINARY INCOME	$		
OTHER INCOME	$		
OTHER EXPENSES	$		
NET INCOME	$		

BUSINESS NAME

PROFIT AND LOSS STATEMENT – DATE: TO			
	$		$
	$		$
	$		$
	$		$
	$		$
TOTAL REVENUES	$		
COST OF GOODS SOLD	$		
GROSS PROFIT	$		
OPERATING EXPENSES			
ADVERTISING	$		
AMORTIZATION	$		
AUTOMOBILE EXPENSES	$		
CHARITABLE CONTRIBUTIONS	$		
DEPRECIATION	$		
EQUIPMENT RENTAL	$		
INSURANCE	$		
INTEREST EXPENSE	$		
LICENSES	$		
OFFICE SUPPLIES	$		
OFFICER COMPENSATION	$		
PAYROLL EXPENSES	$		
RENT	$		
TELEPHONE	$		
TRAVEL & ENTERTAINMENT	$		
UTILITIES	$		
WASTE DISPOSAL	$		
TOTAL OPERATING EXPENSE	$		
NET ORDINARY INCOME	$		
OTHER INCOME	$		
OTHER EXPENSES	$		
NET INCOME	$		

BUSINESS NAME

PROFIT AND LOSS STATEMENT – DATE: TO				
REVENUES				
	$		$	
	$		$	
	$		$	
	$		$	
	$		$	
TOTAL REVENUES	$			
COST OF GOODS SOLD	$			
GROSS PROFIT	$			
OPERATING EXPENSES				
ADVERTISING	$			
AMORTIZATION	$			
AUTOMOBILE EXPENSES	$			
CHARITABLE CONTRIBUTIONS	$			
DEPRECIATION	$			
EQUIPMENT RENTAL	$			
INSURANCE	$			
INTEREST EXPENSE	$			
LICENSES	$			
OFFICE SUPPLIES	$			
OFFICER COMPENSATION	$			
PAYROLL EXPENSES	$			
RENT	$			
TELEPHONE	$			
TRAVEL & ENTERTAINMENT	$			
UTILITIES	$			
WASTE DISPOSAL	$			
TOTAL OPERATING EXPENSE	$			
NET ORDINARY INCOME	$			
OTHER INCOME	$			
OTHER EXPENSES	$			
NET INCOME	$			

BUSINESS NAME

PROFIT AND LOSS STATEMENT – DATE: TO			
REVENUES			
	$		$
	$		$
	$		$
	$		$
	$		$
TOTAL REVENUES	$		
COST OF GOODS SOLD	$		
GROSS PROFIT	$		
OPERATING EXPENSES			
ADVERTISING	$		
AMORTIZATION	$		
AUTOMOBILE EXPENSES	$		
CHARITABLE CONTRIBUTIONS	$		
DEPRECIATION	$		
EQUIPMENT RENTAL	$		
INSURANCE	$		
INTEREST EXPENSE	$		
LICENSES	$		
OFFICE SUPPLIES.	$		
OFFICER COMPENSATION	$		
PAYROLL EXPENSES	$		
RENT	$		
TELEPHONE	$		
TRAVEL & ENTERTAINMENT	$		
UTILITIES	$		
WASTE DISPOSAL	$		
TOTAL OPERATING EXPENSE	$		
NET ORDINARY INCOME	$		
OTHER INCOME	$		
OTHER EXPENSES	$		
NET INCOME	$		

BUSINESS NAME

PROFIT AND LOSS STATEMENT – DATE: TO		
REVENUES		
	$		$
	$		$
	$		$
	$		$
	$		$
TOTAL REVENUES	$	
COST OF GOODS SOLD	$	
GROSS PROFIT	$	
OPERATING EXPENSES		
ADVERTISING	$	
AMORTIZATION	$	
AUTOMOBILE EXPENSES	$	
CHARITABLE CONTRIBUTIONS	$	
DEPRECIATION	$	
EQUIPMENT RENTAL	$	
INSURANCE	$	
INTEREST EXPENSE	$	
LICENSES	$	
OFFICE SUPPLIES	$	
OFFICER COMPENSATION	$	
PAYROLL EXPENSES	$	
RENT	$	
TELEPHONE	$	
TRAVEL & ENTERTAINMENT	$	
UTILITIES	$	
WASTE DISPOSAL	$	
TOTAL OPERATING EXPENSE	$	
NET ORDINARY INCOME	$	
OTHER INCOME	$	
OTHER EXPENSES	$	
NET INCOME	$	

THANK YOU FOR PURCHASING THIS BOOK. WE HOPE YOU WILL FIND IT USEFUL IN YOUR BUSINESS ENTERPRISE.

LOOK FOR OUR OTHER BOOKS DESIGNED TO HELP YOU KEEP TRACK OF WHAT IS GOING ON WITH YOUR BUSINESS!

www.ingramcontent.com/pod-product-compliance
Lightning Source LLC
Chambersburg PA
CBHW080550220526
45466CB00010B/3097